San Francisco Giants 2021

A Baseball Companion

Edited by Steven Goldman and Bret Sayre

Baseball Prospectus

Craig Brown, Associate Editor
Robert Au, Harry Pavlidis and Amy Pircher, Statistics Editors

Copyright © 2021 by DIY Baseball, LLC.
All rights reserved

This book or any part thereof may not be reproduced or transmitted in any form or by any means, electronic or mechanical, including photocopying, recording, or by any information storage and retrieval system, without permission in writing from the publisher.

Limit of Liability/Disclaimer of Warranty: While the publisher and the author have used their best efforts in preparing this book, they make no representations or warranties with respect to the accuracy or completeness of the contents of this book and specifically disclaim any implied warranties of merchantability or fitness for a particular purpose. No warranty may be created or extended by sales representatives or written sales materials. The advice and strategies contained herein may not be suitable for your situation. You should consult with a professional where appropriate. Neither the publisher nor the author shall be liable for any loss of profit or any other commercial damages, including but not limited to special, incidental, consequential, or other damages.

Library of Congress Cataloging-in-Publication Data:
paperback
ISBN-13: 978-1-950716-71-5

Project Credits
Cover Design: Ginny Searle
Interior Design and Production: Amy Pircher, Robert Au
Layout: Amy Pircher, Robert Au

Baseball icon courtesy of Uberux, from https://www.shareicon.net/author/uberux

Ballpark diagram courtesy of Lou Spirito/THIRTY81 Project, https://thirty81project.com/

Manufactured in the United States of America
10 9 8 7 6 5 4 3 2 1

Table of Contents

Statistical Introduction v

Part 1: Team Analysis

Performance Graphs 3
2020 Team Performance 4
2021 Team Projections 5
Team Personnel 6
Oracle Park Stats 7
Giants Team Analysis 9

Part 2: Player Analysis

Giants Player Analysis 14
Giants Prospects 99

Part 3: Featured Articles

Giants All-Time Top 10 Players 111
    by Rob Mains

A Taxonomy of 2020 Abnormalities 117
    by Rob Mains

Tranches of WAR 123
    by Russell A. Carleton

Secondhand Sport 129
    by Patrick Dubuque

Steve Dalkowski Dreaming 133
    by Steven Goldman

A Reward For A Functioning Society 137
    by Cory Frontin and Craig Goldstein

Index of Names 141

Statistical Introduction

Sports are, fundamentally, a blend of athletic endeavor and storytelling. Baseball, like any other sport, tells its stories in so many ways: in the arc of a game from the stands or a season from the box scores, in photos, or even in numbers. At Baseball Prospectus, we understand that statistics don't replace observation or any of baseball's stories, but complement everything else that makes the game so much fun.

What stats help us with is with patterns and precision, variance and value. This book can help you learn things you may not see from watching a game or hundred, whether it's the path of a career over time or the breadth of the entire MLB. We'd also never ask you to choose between our numbers and the experience of viewing a game from the cheap seats or the comfort of your home; our publication combines running the numbers with observations and wisdom from some of the brightest minds we can find. But if you *do* want to learn more about the numbers beyond what's on the backs of player jerseys, let us help explain.

Offense

We've revised our methodology for determining batting value. Long-time readers of the book will notice that we've retired True Average in favor of a new metric: Deserved Runs Created Plus (DRC+). Developed by Jonathan Judge and our stats team, this statistic measures everything a player does at the plate–reaching base, hitting for power, making outs, and moving runners over–and puts it on a scale where 100 equals league-average performance. A DRC+ of 150 is terrific, a DRC+ of 100 is average and a DRC+ of 75 means you better be an excellent defender.

DRC+ also does a better job than any of our previous metrics in taking contextual factors into account. The model adjusts for how the park affects performance, but also for things like the talent of the opposing pitcher, value of different types of batted-ball events, league, temperature and other factors. It's able to describe a player's expected offensive contribution than any other statistic we've found over the years, and also does a better job of predicting future performance as well.

The other aspect of run-scoring is baserunning, which we quantify using Baserunning Runs. BRR not only records the value of stolen bases (or getting caught in the act), but also accounts for all the stuff that doesn't show up on the back of a baseball card: a runner's ability to go first to third on a single, or advance on a fly ball.

Defense

Where offensive value is *relatively* easy to identify and understand, defensive value is ... not. Over the past dozen years, the sabermetric community has focused mostly on stats based on zone data: a real-live human person records the type of batted ball and estimated landing location, and models are created that give expected outs. From there, you can compare fielders' actual outs to those expected ones. Simple, right?

Unfortunately, zone data has two major issues. First, zone data is recorded by commercial data providers who keep the raw data private unless you pay for it. (All the statistics we build in this book and on our website use public data as inputs.) That hurts our ability to test assumptions or duplicate results. Second, over the years it has become apparent that there's quite a bit of "noise" in zone-based fielding analysis. Sometimes the conclusions drawn from zone data don't hold up to scrutiny, and sometimes the different data provided by different providers don't look anything alike, giving wildly different results. Sometimes the hard-working professional stringers or scorers might unknowingly inflict unconscious bias into the mix: for example good fielders will often be credited with more expected outs despite the data, and ballparks with high press boxes tend to score more line drives than ones with a lower press box.

Enter our Fielding Runs Above Average (FRAA). For most positions, FRAA is built from play-by-play data, which allows us to avoid the subjectivity found in many other fielding metrics. The idea is this: count how many fielding plays are made by a given player and compare that to expected plays for an average fielder at their position (based on pitcher ground ball tendencies and batter handedness). Then we adjust for park and base-out situations.

When it comes to catchers, our methodology is a little different thanks to the laundry list of responsibilities they're tasked with beyond just, well, catching and throwing the ball. By now you've probably heard about "framing" or the art of making umpires more likely to call balls outside the strike zone for strikes. To put this into one tidy number, we incorporate pitch tracking data (for the years it exists) and adjust for important factors like pitcher, umpire, batter and home-field advantage using a mixed-model approach. This grants us a number for how many strikes the catcher is personally adding to (or subtracting from) his pitchers' performance ... which we then convert to runs added or lost using linear weights.

Framing is one of the biggest parts of determining catcher value, but we also take into account blocking balls from going past, whether a scorer deems it a passed ball or a wild pitch. We use a similar approach—one that really benefits from the pitch tracking data that tells us what ends up in the dirt and what doesn't. We also include a catcher's ability to prevent stolen bases and how well they field balls in play, and *finally* we come up with our FRAA for catchers.

Pitching

Both pitching and fielding make up the half of baseball that isn't run scoring: run prevention. Separating pitching from fielding is a tough task, and most recent pitching analysis has branched off from Voros McCracken's famous (and controversial) statement, "There is little if any difference among major-league pitchers in their ability to prevent hits on balls hit in the field of play." The research of the analytic community has validated this to some extent, and there are a host of "defense-independent" pitching measures that have been developed to try and extract the effect of the defense behind a hurler from the pitcher's work.

Our solution to this quandary is Deserved Run Average (DRA), our core pitching metric. DRA seeks to evaluate a pitcher's performance, much like earned run average (ERA), the tried-and-true pitching stat you've seen on every baseball broadcast or box score from the past century, but it's very different. To start, DRA takes an event-by-event look at what the pitchers does, and adjusts the value of that event based on different environmental factors like park, batter, catcher, umpire, base-out situation, run differential, inning, defense, home field advantage, pitcher role and temperature. That mixed model gives us a pitcher's expected contribution, similar to what we do for our DRC+ model for hitters and FRAA model for catchers. (Oh, and we also consider the pitcher's effect on basestealing and on balls getting past the catcher.)

DRA is set to the scale of runs allowed per nine innings (RA9) instead of ERA, which makes DRA's scale slightly higher than ERA's. Because of this, for ease of use, we're supplying DRA-, which is much easier for the reader to parse. As with DRC+, DRA- is an "index" stat, meaning instead of using some arbitrary and shifting number to denote what's "good," average is always 100. The reason that it uses a minus rather than a plus is because like ERA, a lower number is better. Therefore a 75 DRA- describes a performance 25 percent better than average, whereas a 150 DRA- means that either a pitcher is getting extremely lucky with their results, or getting ready to try a new pitch.

Since the last time you picked up an edition of this book, we've also made a few minor changes to DRA to make it better. Recent research into "tunneling"—the act of throwing consecutive pitches that appear similar from a batter's point of view until after the swing decision point–data has given us a new contextual factor to account for in DRA: plate distance. This refers to the distance between successive pitches as they approach the plate, and while it has a smaller effect than factors like velocity or whiff rate, it still can help explain pitcher strikeout rate in our model.

Recently Added Descriptive Statistics

Returning to our 2021 edition of the book are a few figures which recently appeared. These numbers may be a little bit more familiar to those of you who have spent some time investigating baseball statistics.

Fastball Percentage

Our fastball percentage (FA%) statistic measures how frequently a pitcher throws a pitch classified as a "fastball," measured as a percentage of overall pitches thrown. We qualify three types of fastballs:

1. The traditional four-seam fastball;
2. The two-seam fastball or sinker;
3. "Hard cutters," which are pitches that have the movement profile of a cut fastball and are used as the pitcher's primary offering or in place of a more traditional fastball.

For example, a pitcher with a FA% of 67 throws any combination of these three pitches about two-thirds of the time.

Whiff Rate

Everybody loves a swing and a miss, and whiff rate (Whiff%) measures how frequently pitchers induce a swinging strike. To calculate Whiff%, we add up all the pitches thrown that ended with a swinging strike, then divide that number by a pitcher's total pitches thrown. Most often, high whiff rates correlate with high strikeout rates (and overall effective pitcher performance).

Called Strike Probability

Called Strike Probability (CSP) is a number that represents the likelihood that all of a pitcher's pitches will be called a strike while controlling for location, pitcher and batter handedness, umpire and count. Here's how it works: on each pitch, our model determines how many times (out of 100) that a similar pitch was called for a strike given those factors mentioned above, and when normalized for each batter's strike zone. Then we average the CSP for all pitches thrown by a pitcher in a season, and that gives us the yearly CSP percentage you see in the stats boxes.

As you might imagine, pitchers with a higher CSP are more likely to work in the zone, where pitchers with a lower CSP are likely locating their pitches outside the normal strike zone, for better or for worse.

Projections

Many of you aren't turning to this book just for a look at what a player has done, but for a look at what a player is going to do: the PECOTA projections. PECOTA, initially developed by Nate Silver (who has moved on to greater fame as a political analyst), consists of three parts:

1. Major-league equivalencies, which use minor-league statistics to project how a player will perform in the major leagues;
2. Baseline forecasts, which use weighted averages and regression to the mean to estimate a player's current true talent level; and
3. Aging curves, which uses the career paths of comparable players to estimate how a player's statistics are likely to change over time.

With all those important things covered, let's take a look at what's in the book this year.

Team Prospectus

Most of this book is composed of team chapters, with one for each of the 30 major-league franchises. On the first page of each chapter, you'll see a box that contains some of the key statistics for each team as well as a very inviting stadium diagram.

We start with the team name, their unadjusted 2020 win-loss record, and their divisional ranking. Beneath that are a host of other team statistics. **Pythag** presents an adjusted 2020 winning percentage, calculated by taking runs scored per game (**RS/G**) and runs allowed per game (**RA/G**) for the team, and running them through a version of Bill James' Pythagorean formula that was refined and improved by David Smyth and Brandon Heipp. (The formula is called "Pythagenpat," which is equally fun to type and to say.)

Next up is **DRC+**, described earlier, to indicate the overall hitting ability of the team either above or below league-average. Run prevention on the pitching side is covered by **DRA** (also mentioned earlier) and another metric: Fielding Independent Pitching (**FIP**), which calculates another ERA-like statistic based on strikeouts, walks, and home runs recorded. Defensive Efficiency Rating (**DER**) tells us the percentage of balls in play turned into outs for the team, and is a quick fielding shorthand that rounds out run prevention.

After that, we have several measures related to roster composition, as opposed to on-field performance. **B-Age** and **P-Age** tell us the average age of a team's batters and pitchers, respectively. **Payroll** is the combined team payroll for all on-field players, and Doug Pappas' Marginal Dollars per Marginal Win (**M$/MW**) tells us how much money a team spent to earn production above replacement level.

San Francisco Giants 2021

Next to each of these stats, we've listed each team's MLB rank in that category from first to 30th. In this, first always indicates a positive outcome and 30th a negative outcome, except in the case of salary—first is highest.

After the franchise statistics, we share a few items about the team's home ballpark. There's the aforementioned diagram of the park's dimensions (including distances to the outfield wall), a graphic showing the height of the wall from the left-field pole to the right-field pole, and a table showing three-year park factors for the stadium. The park factors are displayed as indexes where 100 is average, 110 means that the park inflates the statistic in question by 10 percent, and 90 means that the park deflates the statistic in question by 10 percent.

On the second page of each team chapter, you'll find three graphs. The first is **Payroll History** and helps you see how the team's payroll has compared to the MLB and divisional average payrolls over time. Payroll figures are current as of January 1, 2021; with so many free agents still unsigned as of this writing, the final 2021 figure will likely be significantly different for many teams. (In the meantime, you can always find the most current data at Baseball Prospectus' Cot's Baseball Contracts page.)

The second graph is **Future Commitments** and helps you see the team's future outlays, if any.

The third graph is **Farm System Ranking** and displays how the Baseball Prospectus prospect team has ranked the organization's farm system since 2007.

After the graphs, we have a **Personnel** section that lists many of the important decision-makers and upper-level field and operations staff members for the franchise, as well as any former Baseball Prospectus staff members who are currently part of the organization. (In very rare circumstances, someone might be on both lists!)

Position Players

After all that information and a thoughtful bylined essay covering each team, we present our player comments. These are also bylined, but due to frequent franchise shifts during the offseason, our bylines are more a rough guide than a perfect accounting of who wrote what.

Each player is listed with the major-league team that employed him as of early January 2021. If a player changed teams after that point via free agency, trade, or any other method, you'll be able to find them in the chapter for their previous squad.

As an example, take a look at the player comment for Padres shortstop Fernando Tatis Jr.: the stat block that accompanies his written comment is at the top of this page. First we cover biographical information (age is as of June 30, 2021) before moving onto the stats themselves. Our statistic columns include standard identifying information like **YEAR**, **TEAM**, **LVL** (level of affiliated play) and **AGE** before getting into the numbers. Next, we provide raw, untranslated

Fernando Tatis Jr. SS

Born: 01/02/99 Age: 22 Bats: R Throws: R
Height: 6'3" Weight: 217 Origin: International Free Agent, 2015

YEAR	TEAM	LVL	AGE	PA	R	2B	3B	HR	RBI	BB	K	SB	CS	AVG/OBP/SLG
2018	SA	AA	19	394	77	22	4	16	43	33	109	16	5	.286/.355/.507
2019	SD	MLB	20	372	61	13	6	22	53	30	110	16	6	.317/.379/.590
2020	SD	MLB	21	257	50	11	2	17	45	27	61	11	3	.277/.366/.571
2021 FS	SD	MLB	22	600	95	24	4	31	81	50	165	17	8	.263/.331/.499
2021 DC	SD	MLB	22	628	100	25	4	32	85	53	173	19	8	.263/.331/.499

Comparables: Darryl Strawberry, Bo Bichette, Ronald Acuña Jr.

YEAR	TEAM	LVL	AGE	PA	DRC+	BABIP	BRR	FRAA	WARP
2018	SA	AA	19	394	136	.370	3.0	SS(83): -1.9	2.4
2019	SD	MLB	20	372	118	.410	7.1	SS(83): 0.9	3.4
2020	SD	MLB	21	257	126	.306	0.7	SS(57): -5.5	0.9
2021 FS	SD	MLB	22	600	126	.318	1.7	SS -1	3.9
2021 DC	SD	MLB	22	628	126	.318	1.8	SS -1	4.0

numbers like you might find on the back of your dad's baseball cards: **PA** (plate appearances), **R** (runs), **2B** (doubles), **3B** (triples), **HR** (home runs), **RBI** (runs batted in), **BB** (walks), **K** (strikeouts), **SB** (stolen bases) and **CS** (caught stealing).

Following the basic stats is **Whiff%** (whiff rate), which denotes how often, when a batter swings, he fails to make contact with the ball. Another way to think of this number is an inverse of a hitter's contact rate.

Next, we have unadjusted "slash" statistics: **AVG** (batting average), **OBP** (on-base percentage) and **SLG** (slugging percentage). Following the slash line is **DRC+** (Deserved Runs Created Plus), which we described earlier as total offensive expected contribution compared to the league average.

BABIP (batting average on balls in play) tells us how often a ball in play fell for a hit, and can help us identify whether a batter may have been lucky or not ... but note that high BABIPs also tend to follow the great hitters of our time, as well as speedy singles hitters who put the ball on the ground.

The next item is **BRR** (Baserunning Runs), which covers all of a player's baserunning accomplishments including (but not limited to) swiped bags and failed attempts. Next is **FRAA** (Fielding Runs Above Average), which also includes the number of games previously played at each position noted in parentheses. Multi-position players have only their two most frequent positions listed here, but their total FRAA number reflects all positions played.

Our last column here is **WARP** (Wins Above Replacement Player). WARP estimates the total value of a player, which means for hitters it takes into account hitting runs above average (calculated using the DRC+ model), BRR and FRAA. Then, it makes an adjustment for positions played and gives the player a credit for plate appearances based upon the difference between "replacement level"—which is derived from the quality of players added to a team's roster after the start of the season–and the league average.

The final line just below the stats box is **PECOTA** data, which is discussed further in a following section.

Catchers

Catchers are a special breed, and thus they have earned their own separate box which displays some of the defensive metrics that we've built just for them. As an example, let's check out Yasmani Grandal.

YEAR	TEAM	P. COUNT	FRM RUNS	BLK RUNS	THRW RUNS	TOT RUNS
2018	LAD	16816	15.7	0.8	0.1	16.5
2019	MIL	18740	19.4	1.8	-0.1	21.1
2020	CHW	4830	3.7	0.3	-0.2	3.8
2021	CHW	14430	16.7	-0.6	1.0	17.1
2021	CHW	14430	16.7	0.4	1.0	18.0

The **YEAR** and **TEAM** columns match what you'd find in the other stat box. **P. COUNT** indicates the number of pitches thrown while the catcher was behind the plate, including swinging strikes, fouls and balls in play. **FRM RUNS** is the total run value the catcher provided (or cost) his team by influencing the umpire to call strikes where other catchers did not. **BLK RUNS** expresses the total run value above or below average for the catcher's ability to prevent wild pitches and passed balls. **THRW RUNS** is calculated using a similar model as the previous two statistics, and it measures a catcher's ability to throw out basestealers but also to dissuade them from testing his arm in the first place. It takes into account factors like the pitcher (including his delivery and pickoff move) and baserunner (who could be as fast as Billy Hamilton or as slow as Yonder Alonso). **TOT RUNS** is the sum of all of the previous three statistics.

Pitchers

Let's give our pitchers a turn, using 2020 AL Cy Young winner Shane Bieber as our example. Take a look at his stat block: the first line and the **YEAR**, **TEAM**, **LVL** and **AGE** columns are the same as in the position player example earlier.

Here too, we have a series of columns that display raw, unadjusted statistics compiled by the pitcher over the course of a season: **W** (wins), **L** (losses), **SV** (saves), **G** (games pitched), **GS** (games started), **IP** (innings pitched), **H** (hits allowed) and **HR** (home runs allowed). Next we have two statistics that are rates: **BB/9** (walks per nine innings) and **K/9** (strikeouts per nine innings), before returning to the unadjusted **K** (strikeouts).

Next up is **GB%** (ground ball percentage), which is the percentage of all batted balls that were hit on the ground, including both outs and hits. Remember, this is based on observational data and subject to human error, so please approach this with a healthy dose of skepticism.

BABIP (batting average on balls in play) is calculated using the same methodology as it is for position players, but it often tells us more about a pitcher than it does a hitter. With pitchers, a high BABIP is often due to poor defense or bad luck, and can often be an indicator of potential rebound, and a low BABIP may be cause to expect performance regression. (A typical league-average BABIP is close to .290-.300.)

The metrics **WHIP** (walks plus hits per inning pitched) and **ERA** (earned run average) are old standbys: WHIP measures walks and hits allowed on a per-inning basis, while ERA measures earned runs on a nine-inning basis. Neither of these stats are translated or adjusted.

DRA- (Deserved Run Average) was described at length earlier, and measures how the pitcher "deserved" to perform compared to other pitchers. Please note that since we lack all the data points that would make for a "real" DRA for minor-league events, the DRA- displayed for minor league partial-seasons is based off of different data. (That data is a modified version of our cFIP metric, which you can find more information about on our website.)

Shane Bieber   RHP

Born: 05/31/95   Age: 26   Bats: R   Throws: R
Height: 6'3"   Weight: 200   Origin: Round 4, 2016 Draft (#122 overall)

YEAR	TEAM	LVL	AGE	W	L	SV	G	GS	IP	H	HR	BB/9	K/9	K	GB%	BABIP
2018	AKR	AA	23	3	0	0	5	5	31	26	1	0.3	8.7	30	47.3%	.278
2018	COL	AAA	23	3	1	0	8	8	48^2	30	3	1.1	8.7	47	52.0%	.227
2018	CLE	MLB	23	11	5	0	20	19	114^2	130	13	1.8	9.3	118	46.2%	.356
2019	CLE	MLB	24	15	8	0	34	33	214^1	186	31	1.7	10.9	259	44.4%	.298
2020	CLE	MLB	25	8	1	0	12	12	77^1	46	7	2.4	14.2	122	48.4%	.267
2021 FS	CLE	MLB	26	10	6	0	26	26	150	121	18	2.1	11.7	195	45.5%	.297
2021 DC	CLE	MLB	26	14	7	0	30	30	196.7	159	24	2.1	11.7	257	45.5%	.297

Comparables: Luis Severino, Danny Salazar, Joe Musgrove

YEAR	TEAM	LVL	AGE	WHIP	ERA	DRA-	WARP	MPH	FB%	WHF	CSP
2018	AKR	AA	23	0.87	1.16	61	0.9				
2018	COL	AAA	23	0.74	1.66	69	1.2				
2018	CLE	MLB	23	1.33	4.55	74	2.6	94.7	57.4%	26.2%	
2019	CLE	MLB	24	1.05	3.28	75	4.9	94.4	45.8%	30.8%	
2020	CLE	MLB	25	0.87	1.63	53	2.6	95.3	53.6%	40.7%	
2021 FS	CLE	MLB	26	1.04	2.44	64	4.4	94.7	50.0%	33.2%	44.2%
2021 DC	CLE	MLB	26	1.04	2.44	64	5.8	94.7	50.0%	33.2%	44.2%

Just like with hitters, **WARP** (Wins Above Replacement Player) is a total value metric that puts pitchers of all stripes on the same scale as position players. We use DRA as the primary input for our calculation of WARP. You might notice that relief pitchers (due to their limited innings) may have a lower WARP than you were expecting or than you might see in other WARP-like metrics. WARP does not take leverage into account, just the actions a pitcher performs and the expected value of those actions ... which ends up judging high-leverage relief pitchers differently than you might imagine given their prestige and market value.

MPH gives you the pitcher's 95th percentile velocity for the noted season, in order to give you an idea of what the *peak* fastball velocity a pitcher possesses. Since this comes from our pitch-tracking data, it is not publicly available for minor-league pitchers.

Finally, we display the three new pitching metrics we described earlier. **FB%** (fastball percentage) gives you the percentage of fastballs thrown out of all pitches. **WHF** (whiff rate) tells you the percentage of swinging strikes induced out of all pitches. **CSP** (called strike probability) expresses the likelihood of all pitches thrown to result in a called strike, after controlling for factors like handedness, umpire, pitch type, count and location.

PECOTA

All players have PECOTA projections for 2021, as well as a set of other numbers that describe the performance of comparable players according to PECOTA. All projections for 2021 are for the player at the date we went to press in early January and are projected into the league and park context as indicated by the team abbreviation. (Note that players at very low levels of the minors are too unpredictable to assess using these numbers.) All PECOTA projected statistics represent a player's projected major-league performance.

How we're doing that is a little different this season. There are really two different values that go into the final stat line that you see for PECOTA: How a player performs, and how much playing time he'll be given to perform it. In the past we've estimated playing time based on each team's roster and depth charts, and we'll continue to do that. These projections are denoted as **2021 DC**.

But in many cases, a player won't be projected for major-league playing time; most of the time this is because they aren't projected to be major-league players at all, but still developing as prospects. Or perhaps a player will provide Triple-A depth, only to have an opportunity open up because of injury. For these purposes, we're also supplying a second projection, labeled **2021 FS**, or full season. This is what we would project the player to provide in 600 plate appearances or 150 innings pitched.

Below the projections are the player's three highest-scoring comparable players as determined by PECOTA. All comparables represent a snapshot of how the listed player was performing at the same age as the current player, so if a

23-year-old pitcher is compared to Bartolo Colón, he's actually being compared to a 23-year-old Colón, not the version that pitched for the Rangers in 2018, nor to Colón's career as a whole.

A few points about pitcher projections. First, we aren't yet projecting peak velocity, so that column will be blank in the PECOTA lines. Second, projecting DRA is trickier than evaluating past performance, because it is unclear how deserving each pitcher will be of his anticipated outcomes. However, we know that another DRA-related statistic–contextual FIP or cFIP-estimates future run scoring very well. So for PECOTA, the projected DRA- figures you see are based on the past cFIPs generated by the pitcher and comparable players over time, along with the other factors described above.

If you're familiar with PECOTA, then you'll have noticed that the projection system often appears bullish on players coming off a bad year and bearish on players coming off a good year. (This is because the system weights several previous seasons, not just the most recent one.) In addition, we publish the 50th percentile projections for each player–which is smack in the middle of the range of projected production—which tends to mean PECOTA stat lines don't often have extreme results like 40 home runs or 250 strikeouts in a given season. In essence, PECOTA doesn't project very many extreme seasons.

Managers

After all those wonderful team chapters, we've got statistics for each big-league manager, all of whom are organized by alphabetical order. Here you'll find a block including an extraordinary amount of information collected from each manager's entire career. For more information on the acronyms and what they mean, please visit the Glossary at www.baseballprospectus.com.

There is one important metric that we'd like to call attention to, and you'll find it next to each manager's name: **wRM+** (weighted reliever management plus). Developed by Rob Arthur and Rian Watt, wRM+ investigates how good a manager is at using their best relievers during the moments of highest leverage, using both our proprietary DRA metric as well as Leverage Index. wRM+ is scaled to a league average of 100, and a wRM+ of 105 indicates that relievers were used approximately five percent "better" than average. On the other hand, a wRM+ of 95 would tell us the team used its relievers five percent "worse" than the average team.

While wRM+ does not have an extremely strong correlation with a manager, it is statistically significant; this means that a manager is not *entirely* responsible for a team's wRM+, but does have some effect on that number.

Part 1: Team Analysis

Performance Graphs

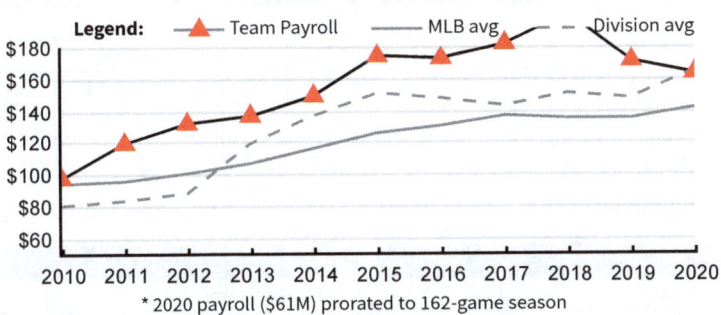

Payroll History (in millions)

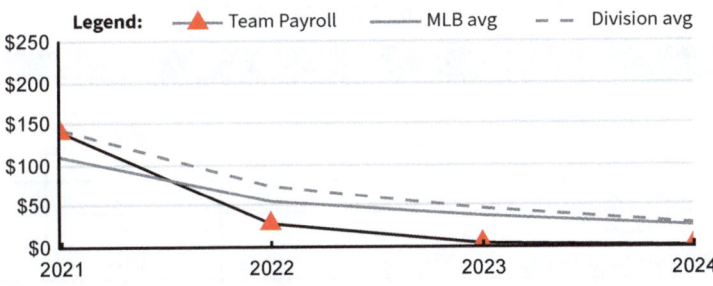

Future Commitments (in millions)

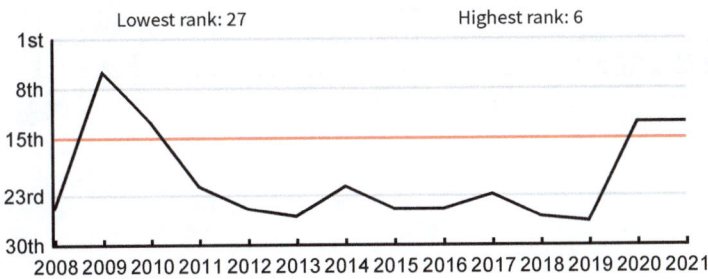

Farm System Ranking

2020 Team Performance

ACTUAL STANDINGS

Team	W	L	Pct
LAD	43	17	0.717
SD	37	23	0.617
SF	**29**	**31**	**0.483**
COL	26	34	0.433
ARI	25	35	0.417

dWIN% STANDINGS

Team	W	L	Pct
LAD	37	23	0.624
SD	34	26	0.567
SF	**27**	**33**	**0.465**
ARI	23	37	0.386
COL	22	38	0.375

TOP HITTERS

Player	WARP
Mike Yastrzemski	1.7
Brandon Belt	1.4
Wilmer Flores	0.9

TOP PITCHERS

Player	WARP
Kevin Gausman	1.4
Drew Smyly	0.7
Logan Webb	0.6

VITAL STATISTICS

Statistic Name	Value	Rank
Pythagenpat	.503	13th
dWin%	.465	15th
Runs Scored per Game	4.98	8th
Runs Allowed per Game	4.95	18th
Deserved Runs Created Plus	105	5th
Deserved Run Average Minus	105	21st
Fielding Independent Pitching	4.47	16th
Defensive Efficiency Rating	.703	15th
Batter Age	30.4	30th
Pitcher Age	29.5	25th
Payroll	$61.0M	13th
Marginal $ per Marginal Win	$3.9M	16th

2021 Team Projections

PROJECTED STANDINGS

Team	W	L	Pct	+/-
LAD	104.4	57.6	0.644	-11
With Dustin May ready and David Price returning, adding Trevor Bauer was purely lapidary. Still, they're almost alone in their willingness to put up or shut up.				
SD	95.4	66.6	0.589	-4
Not just Blake Snell, but Yu Darvish and Joe Musgrove; not just Ha-Seong Kim, but Jurickson Profar, all without trading a starting player.				
ARI	79.2	82.8	0.489	11
Mike Hazen is a good trader, but ownership continues to confine him to corner-store bartering.				
SF	**74.9**	**87.1**	**0.462**	**-3**
Most of their individual moves were small, but the Giants' winter work amounts to the first step toward pivoting from a rebuild to contending.				
COL	58.9	103.1	0.364	-11
The time was ripe for a rebuild, but the return for Nolan Arenado is not a confidence-inspiring start.				

TOP PROJECTED HITTERS

Player	WARP
Mike Yastrzemski	3.4
Tommy La Stella	2.3
Brandon Belt	2.3

TOP PROJECTED PITCHERS

Player	WARP
Kevin Gausman	2.5
Alex Wood	1.8
Johnny Cueto	1.4

FARM SYSTEM REPORT

Top Prospect	Number of Top 101 Prospects
Marco Luciano, #8	4

KEY DEDUCTIONS

Player	WARP
Drew Smyly	1.1
Daniel Robertson	0.5
Shaun Anderson	0.3

KEY ADDITIONS

Player	WARP
Buster Posey	2.3
Tommy La Stella	2.3
Alex Wood	1.8
Anthony DeSclafani	1.2
Curt Casali	0.6
Matt Wisler	0.5
LaMonte Wade Jr	0.3
John Brebbia	0.3

Team Personnel

President of Baseball Operations
Farhan Zaidi

Executive Vice President of Baseball Operations
Brian Sabean

General Manager
Scott Harris

Vice President & Assistant General Manager
Jeremy Shelley

Vice President of Baseball Operations
Yeshayah Goldfarb

Manager
Gabe Kapler

Oracle Park Stats

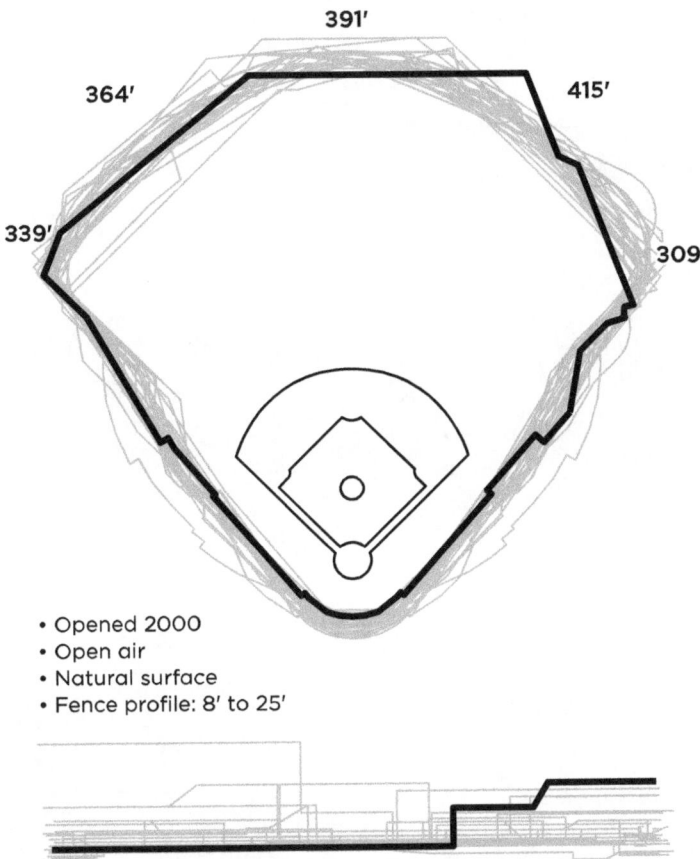

- Opened 2000
- Open air
- Natural surface
- Fence profile: 8' to 25'

Three-Year Park Factors

Runs	Runs/RH	Runs/LH	HR/RH	HR/LH
94	95	91	87	81

Giants Team Analysis

Ten years ago, when my age started with "30-something", rather than "40-something", the San Francisco Giants were basking in the glow of what was their first World Series title since moving to California. We know what happened next. The Giants missed the playoffs in 2011, but won the 2012 World Series, missed the playoffs in 2013, and then won the 2014 World Series. Having once again missed the playoffs the year prior, the 2016 Giants struggled back in Game 3 of the NLDS against the Cubs, managing to win in 13 innings, then lead Game 4 by three in the ninth, allowing, for a brief moment, the even-year magic potion to seem strangely real. But as the Cubs scored four runs in the top of the inning and eventually became the first non-Giants even-year champs since the 2008 Phillies, everyone preemptively declared them to be a dynasty.

Chances are that the person reading this essay is a Giants fan—we know that you flip to your favorite team first—and so when I say the word "dynasty", you might be a little more willing to apply it to those teams of a decade or so ago. But there are some of you who are just "fans of the game" reading this one who might be looking back and find yourself saying, "Oh yeah, I guess that was a dynasty" In fact, you're more likely to apply the "D word" to the Cubs and their good-but-never-quite-fulfilled run in the second half of the 2010s.

But then since 2017, the Giants seemed to have left their hearts somewhere else. The 2020 season marked their fourth consecutive losing campaign, meaning that a Giants fan in Merced just went through the entirety of high school without seeing a winning team. It's not like 2021 promises to be all that much better. There is talent coming up on the farm, but this is the year of transition to the new generation and most of the old guard will be departing. Madison Bumgarner has already decamped for Arizona. Hunter Pence finally learned to parallel park and retired. Brian Wilson is back to singing Beach Boys songs. And this will be the final ride for the Brandons, Belt and Crawford, and perhaps even Buster Posey, who has a $22 million team option for 2022.

Posey's place in Giants lore is secure and the bat is still there so that even if he becomes a serviceable first baseman for a few years, that'll be good enough to pick up a few more career WARP and get into the Hall of Fame on the Joe Mauer path—particularly if those last years are all with the Giants. But the Brandons have both been mainstays of the team for most of a decade. And like the Giants overall, I don't think they've ever gotten their due as to how important and valuable they have been over the years.

Belt, in particular, always seemed to never quite connect. A decade ago in our *Baseball Prospectus* annual, he was described as "flat-out Ruthian" in the minor leagues. Now that the flower has bloomed, we find that Belt has had an above-average OBP and excellent defense at first and some "doubles power," but to date has never had a 20-home run season. It translates into a good, though not overwhelming first base profile. Had Belt been an unheralded prospect who showed up and produced seasons of 0.8, 3.0, 1.3, 2.7, 1.8, 2.1, 1.9, and (in a shortened 2020 season) 1.3 WARP, over the course of eight seasons, that would be seen as a player development marvel. It always seems so much less interesting when it's someone who was supposed to be that 6 WARP per year cornerstone. Crawford didn't have the same hype coming up as a prospect, and has made a career of being a just-below-average hitter, relative to the league, but one who could play a very good version of shortstop. Those who know a little bit about WARP know that's a recipe for a decent player.

Part of the problem is that they are both making in excess of $15 million per year. Had they been young enough to be arb-eligible, that sort of (projected) salary would have probably made them a non-tender candidate. Fifteen million dollars is the sort of salary that, even though we all know the whole "a win has been worth $8 to $10 million in the free agent market over the past few years" thing, feels like it should be attached to someone who provides more value. And I get it. No one will ever make the case that Belt or Crawford are hidden superstars, but it's worth pointing out how valuable a consistently average player is in Major League Baseball.

Warning! Gory Mathematical Details Ahead!
In 2019—I'm going to ignore 2020 because the shortened season makes a mess of these comparisons—there were 127 hitters who posted a WARP of at least 2.0 wins. If you take it down to the level of 1.5 wins, you get 166 hitters. On an average team, players like Belt and Crawford, who have consistently put up WARP scores in that range, settle into the "fourth- or fifth-best overall" range of the eight regular position player starters on the team. They may or may not be the fourth- or fifth-best hitter, because WARP includes defense and baserunning. Belt and Crawford are gloriously average regulars in any given season. Not bad. Not great. Average. Before you consider that too great a curse, read on.

I looked at all position players who logged at least 100 PA in a given season and who debuted after 1996. I looked at all player seasons between 1996 and 2019, again excluding 2020 because of the shortened schedule. Between those years, there were 1,680 unique individuals who logged at least one season of 100 PA, two of whom were Crawford and Belt. During that span, Crawford and Belt both notched six seasons above 1.5 WARP. Not bad. Forty-four other players can make that claim. Where does that place the Brandons in the grand scheme of things?

Number of 1.5 win seasons	Percent of Sample	Cumulative Percentage
0	54.9%	54.9%
1	14.3%	69.3%
2	7.3%	76.5%
3	6.1%	82.7%
4	3.5%	86.2%
5	3.5%	89.7%
6	2.7%	92.4%
7	1.8%	94.3%
8+	5.9%	100.0%

(note: due to rounding, some of the percentages might look a tiny bit off)

If we look at the Brandons from this perspective, looking over their *full body of work* (to date), they are part of the elite 10 percent of their contemporaries who were consistently able to produce boringly average outcomes year after year, even if they never had anything close to an MVP campaign. (If you want to give Belt credit for his 1.3 WARP performance in 2020 over 60 games, he reaches the top six percent.) It doesn't look all that impressive when viewed as a single season, but longevity is its own skill, and one that never gets its proper due when we talk about major leaguers. We love our supernovae, who explode for a season or two, but forget our North Stars quietly sitting there night after night guiding the way.

There will be a few more players—in this sample, the ones who perhaps debuted in 2018 and will eventually cross the line of six seasons of 1.5 WARP or more, but haven't had the chance to do that yet—that will join them in that club, but it won't change the overall conclusion. Brandons Crawford and Belt have played a different role than perhaps Giants' fans had hoped for, but one that was important all along and certainly not one to be sad about.

This coming season might be the last time that fans get to see either one in San Francisco. They're on the wrong side of 30-something, along with a lot of the rest of the team, and that core hasn't been very good lately. Some of you have seen this movie before. The teardown is coming, if it isn't already here. The guard will change. Brian Sabean is already gone, and the Giants got one of those newfangled "analytics" GMs to run the show. This team will probably be built differently than the old one was. Maybe there will eventually be a new dynasty in (Northern) California, but for a little while, those memories of Bumgarner's five innings of relief in 2014 will be the only thing that will keep Giants fans warm at Mega Interwebs Stadium. But as you look back, maybe it's time to appreciate how important the Brandons were to that time period. They've done something that not a lot of players can say that they have. They stuck around.

And I hope that fans will stick around too. There's a talent to sticking through the tough times. Eventually, there will be a resurgence by the Bay, and there's a 50/50 shot that it will happen in an even year. Some new generation of players will start hitting balls into McCovey Cove and eventually they'll have their magic moments. Maybe even one of the Brandons will be around to see them, still chugging along and putting up solid-if-not-spectacular performances. And that will still be valuable.

—*Russell A. Carleton is an author of Baseball Prospectus.*

Part 2: Player Analysis

PLAYER COMMENTS WITH GRAPHS

Joey Bart   C
Born: 12/15/96   Age: 24   Bats: R   Throws: R
Height: 6'2"   Weight: 238   Origin: Round 1, 2018 Draft (#2 overall)

YEAR	TEAM	LVL	AGE	PA	R	2B	3B	HR	RBI	BB	K	SB	CS	AVG/OBP/SLG
2018	GIO	ROK	21	25	3	1	1	0	1	1	7	0	0	.261/.320/.391
2018	SK	SS	21	203	35	14	2	13	39	12	40	2	1	.298/.369/.613
2019	SJ	HI-A	22	251	37	10	2	12	37	14	50	5	2	.265/.315/.479
2019	RIC	AA	22	87	9	4	1	4	11	7	21	0	2	.316/.368/.544
2020	SF	MLB	23	111	15	5	2	0	7	3	41	0	0	.233/.288/.320
2021 FS	SF	MLB	24	600	70	24	5	20	72	31	201	1	2	.224/.279/.398
2021 DC	SF	MLB	24	124	14	5	1	4	14	6	41	0	0	.224/.279/.398

Comparables: Luis Exposito, John Hicks, Jose Lobaton

Bart, a former first-round pick out of Georgia Tech, made his major-league debut in August, an outcome that was likely even if the season had not been derailed by a global pandemic. The wrinkle in this plan, of course, was the lack of early-season reps at Triple-A, which meant throwing Bart into the middle of the strangest of seasons and the unlikeliest of playoff runs. The Giants were probably not surprised by a rocky debut that featured little power and far too many strikeouts at the plate, and a steep defensive learning curve behind it. There's plenty of college and minor-league data suggesting Bart is still the heir apparent to Posey, but the questions raised by his performance were likely enough to confirm that a longer pass through Triple-A may be the best outcome for all concerned.

YEAR	TEAM	P. COUNT	FRM RUNS	BLK RUNS	THRW RUNS	TOT RUNS
2019	RIC	2187	0.4	0.0	0.1	0.5
2020	SF	4088	0.3	0.0	0.2	0.5
2021	SF	4810	1.1	0.3	-0.2	1.2
2021	SF	4810	1.1	0.1	-0.2	0.9

YEAR	TEAM	LVL	AGE	PA	DRC+	BABIP	BRR	FRAA	WARP
2018	GIO	ROK	21	25		.375			
2018	SK	SS	21	203	146	.318	1.2	C(32): -1.0	1.0
2019	SJ	HI-A	22	251	112	.291	1.0	C(50): -1.9	1.2
2019	RIC	AA	22	87	163	.382	-1.2	C(15): 0.2	0.8
2020	SF	MLB	23	111	48	.387	-0.5	C(32): 0.1	-0.4
2021 FS	SF	MLB	24	600	85	.309	0.0	C 4	1.7
2021 DC	SF	MLB	24	124	85	.309	0.0	C 1	0.4

Joey Bart, continued

Batted Ball Distribution

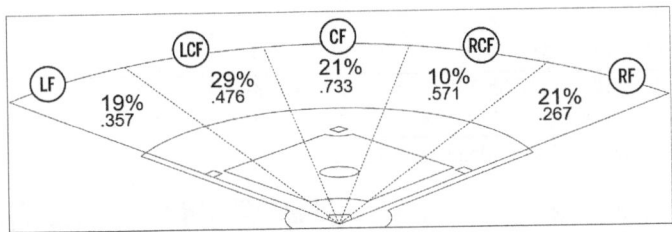

Strike Zone vs LHP

Strike Zone vs RHP

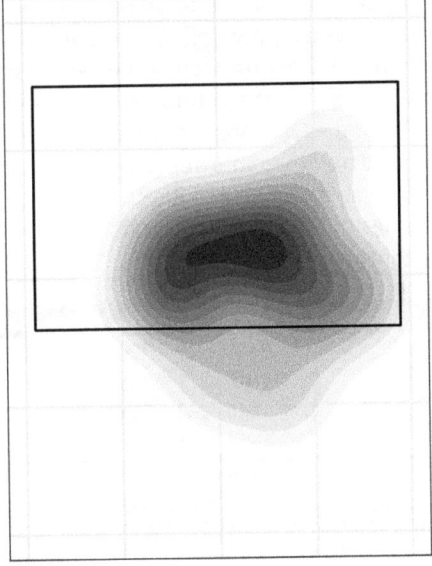

San Francisco Giants 2021

Curt Casali   C

Born: 11/09/88   Age: 32   Bats: R   Throws: R
Height: 6'2"   Weight: 220   Origin: Round 10, 2011 Draft (#317 overall)

YEAR	TEAM	LVL	AGE	PA	R	2B	3B	HR	RBI	BB	K	SB	CS	AVG/OBP/SLG
2018	DUR	AAA	29	104	13	5	0	4	20	7	19	0	0	.274/.327/.453
2018	CIN	MLB	29	156	15	10	0	4	16	12	32	0	2	.293/.355/.450
2019	CIN	MLB	30	236	24	9	0	8	32	25	59	0	0	.251/.331/.411
2020	CIN	MLB	31	93	10	3	0	6	8	14	29	2	0	.224/.366/.500
2021 FS	SF	MLB	32	600	73	18	1	19	68	65	182	1	1	.214/.311/.368
2021 DC	SF	MLB	32	187	22	5	0	6	21	20	56	0	0	.214/.311/.368

Comparables: Tom Wilson, Rich Rowland, Jason LaRue

Casali once again held up his end as the righty/good-hit/decent-frame/poor-block half of Cincinnati's backstop platoon. Among National League catchers only Will Smith and Austin Nola posted a higher DRC+, fueled by Casali's .290/.389/.613 line against southpaws. His worst two offensive seasons occurred when he came to the plate more than 200 times so concerns that the veteran receiver would be overexposed if used in an expanded role, and saw more same-side pitching, are warranted. Good catchers are hard to find and even harder to develop, so Casali's consistent competence and noted game-calling skills should keep him challenging teammates to off-season games of CupCheck for years to come. The Giants snagged him in free agency after the Reds non-tendered Casali in the offseason.

YEAR	TEAM	P. COUNT	FRM RUNS	BLK RUNS	THRW RUNS	TOT RUNS
2018	CIN	4858	-2.1	-1.3	-0.2	-3.5
2019	CIN	8395	4.5	1.8	-0.3	6.0
2020	CIN	3610	1.0	-0.3	0.0	0.7
2021	SF	7215	2.7	-1.4	-0.2	1.1
2021	SF	7215	2.7	-0.9	-0.2	1.6

YEAR	TEAM	LVL	AGE	PA	DRC+	BABIP	BRR	FRAA	WARP
2018	DUR	AAA	29	104	110	.301	-0.1	C(26): 1.0	0.6
2018	CIN	MLB	29	156	101	.352	0.1	C(38): -4.1, 1B(6): 0.1, 2B(1): -0.0	0.3
2019	CIN	MLB	30	236	102	.308	0.1	C(67): 6.0, 1B(4): 0.0	1.8
2020	CIN	MLB	31	93	112	.268	-0.8	C(29): -0.1	0.5
2021 FS	SF	MLB	32	600	91	.286	-0.8	C 2, 1B 0	1.9
2021 DC	SF	MLB	32	187	91	.286	-0.2	C 1	0.6

Curt Casali, continued

Batted Ball Distribution

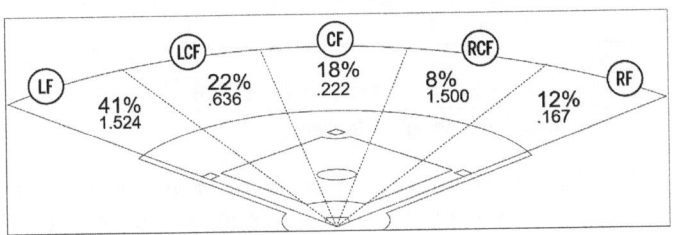

Strike Zone vs LHP   **Strike Zone vs RHP**

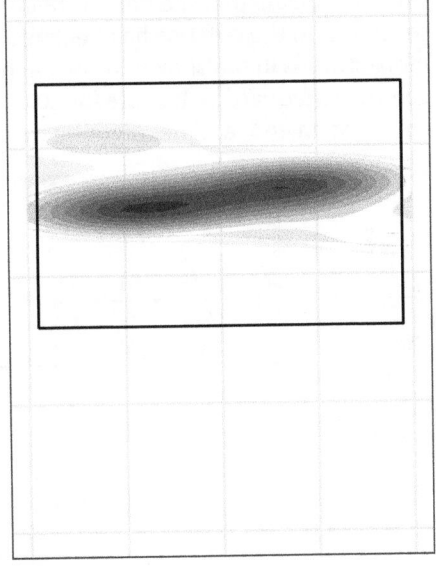

Brandon Crawford SS

Born: 01/21/87 Age: 34 Bats: L Throws: R
Height: 6'1" Weight: 223 Origin: Round 4, 2008 Draft (#117 overall)

YEAR	TEAM	LVL	AGE	PA	R	2B	3B	HR	RBI	BB	K	SB	CS	AVG/OBP/SLG
2018	SF	MLB	31	594	63	28	2	14	54	50	122	4	5	.254/.325/.394
2019	SF	MLB	32	560	58	24	2	11	59	53	117	3	2	.228/.304/.350
2020	SF	MLB	33	193	26	12	0	8	28	15	47	1	2	.256/.326/.465
2021 FS	SF	MLB	34	600	66	25	3	14	67	50	147	5	2	.228/.302/.371
2021 DC	SF	MLB	34	445	49	18	2	11	50	37	109	3	2	.228/.302/.371

Comparables: Chris Woodward, Cliff Pennington, Jay Bell

    The long tail of Crawford's career is aging about as well as his flowing, wavy, intentionally unkempt, unfailingly moist hair. Depending on your tastes, this could be either insult or compliment. On the plus side, there has scarcely been a more reliable position player in the major leagues over the last decade than Crawford. Since assuming the full-time job during 2012, the second of the Giants' three World Series-winning years, Crawford has played in at least 143 games from 2013 through 2019 (appearing in 54 games in the shortened 2020). Yet, recognizing that the bat has been roughly league-average for several seasons and the defense has declined to merely "good" feels like finding a few more strands in the shower drain each year. There's not enough in the negative column to jeopardize his role for 2021, but after that, Crawford's six-year deal will be at an end, and he might be overdue for a cut.

YEAR	TEAM	LVL	AGE	PA	DRC+	BABIP	BRR	FRAA	WARP
2018	SF	MLB	31	594	95	.302	0.5	SS(146): 15.3	4.0
2019	SF	MLB	32	560	79	.274	-3.4	SS(142): 0.9	0.9
2020	SF	MLB	33	193	98	.303	-1.7	SS(53): 3.4	0.6
2021 FS	SF	MLB	34	600	86	.285	0.0	SS 2	1.0
2021 DC	SF	MLB	34	445	86	.285	0.0	SS 1	0.7

Brandon Crawford, continued

Batted Ball Distribution

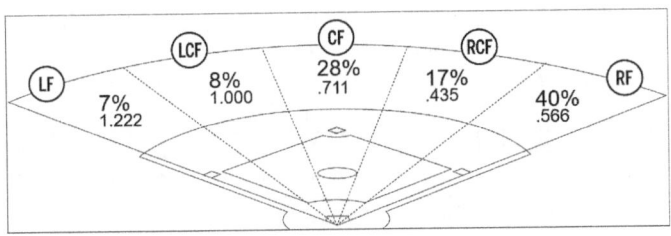

Strike Zone vs LHP   Strike Zone vs RHP

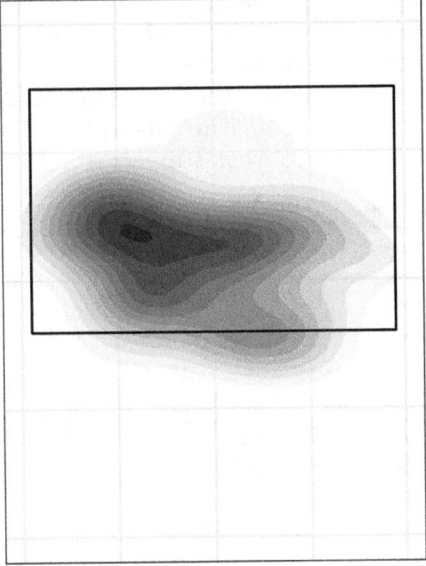

San Francisco Giants 2021

Mauricio Dubón SS
Born: 07/19/94 Age: 26 Bats: R Throws: R
Height: 6'0" Weight: 173 Origin: Round 26, 2013 Draft (#773 overall)

YEAR	TEAM	LVL	AGE	PA	R	2B	3B	HR	RBI	BB	K	SB	CS	AVG/OBP/SLG
2018	RMV	AAA	23	114	18	9	2	4	18	2	19	6	3	.343/.348/.574
2019	SA	AAA	24	427	59	22	1	16	47	18	59	9	6	.297/.333/.475
2019	SAC	AAA	24	112	23	4	0	4	9	10	9	1	2	.323/.391/.485
2019	MIL	MLB	24	2	0	0	0	0	0	0	1	0	0	.000/.000/.000
2019	SF	MLB	24	109	12	5	0	4	9	5	19	3	1	.279/.312/.442
2020	SF	MLB	25	177	21	4	1	4	19	15	36	2	3	.274/.337/.389
2021 FS	SF	MLB	26	600	69	25	3	16	68	35	123	13	5	.257/.305/.406
2021 DC	SF	MLB	26	530	61	22	3	14	60	31	109	11	5	.257/.305/.406

Comparables: Devon White, Billy Conigliaro, Roberto Kelly

The awkward masonry of the Giants' roster only works with the right type of mortar. Fitting the worn brick of aging players on legacy contracts (Longoria, Belt, Posey) with pieces repurposed from the post-prospect junkyard (Yaz, Slater, Dickerson) demands some multipositional spackle, something flexible and springy enough to survive the inevitable stresses of a rebuilding team. Dubón is the adhesive substance of this slapdash edifice. Bouncing around from second, to shortstop and ultimately finding his best use in center field, Dubón gave the Giants credible defense, passable on-base ability and all the speed you can handle. Even if he'll never be a load-bearing keystone, he can help a team in transition avoid catastrophic structural failure.

YEAR	TEAM	LVL	AGE	PA	DRC+	BABIP	BRR	FRAA	WARP
2018	RMV	AAA	23	114	106	.379	1.5	SS(23): 0.3, 2B(4): 0.6	0.7
2019	SA	AAA	24	427	102	.316	-0.9	SS(83): 4.1, 2B(12): 0.7, 3B(1): -0.0	2.4
2019	SAC	AAA	24	112	102	.326	0.6	SS(17): -0.1, 2B(7): 0.3	0.9
2019	MIL	MLB	24	2	84	.000		SS(1): -0.0	0.0
2019	SF	MLB	24	109	88	.309	1.1	2B(22): 3.8, SS(9): -0.4	0.7
2020	SF	MLB	25	177	96	.328	-0.5	CF(44): 1.3, 2B(8): 0.6, SS(8): -0.1	0.6
2021 FS	SF	MLB	26	600	94	.301	0.9	CF 5, SS 0	2.0
2021 DC	SF	MLB	26	530	94	.301	0.8	CF 5, SS 0	1.9

Mauricio Dubón, continued

Batted Ball Distribution

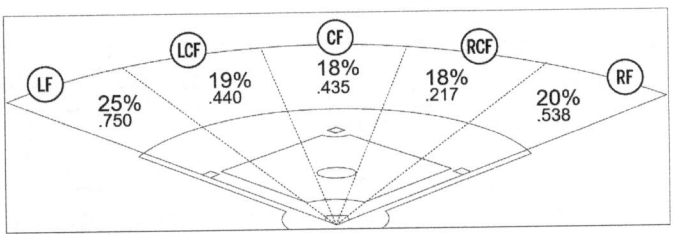

Strike Zone vs LHP

Strike Zone vs RHP

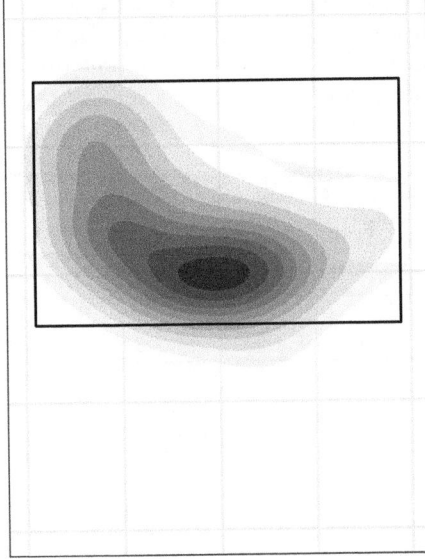

Wilmer Flores 2B

Born: 08/06/91 Age: 29 Bats: R Throws: R
Height: 6'2" Weight: 213 Origin: International Free Agent, 2007

YEAR	TEAM	LVL	AGE	PA	R	2B	3B	HR	RBI	BB	K	SB	CS	AVG/OBP/SLG
2018	NYM	MLB	26	429	43	25	0	11	51	29	42	0	0	.267/.319/.417
2019	ARI	MLB	27	285	31	18	0	9	37	15	31	0	0	.317/.361/.487
2020	SF	MLB	28	213	30	11	1	12	32	13	36	1	0	.268/.315/.515
2021 FS	SF	MLB	29	600	74	25	2	24	83	36	98	1	1	.266/.316/.453
2021 DC	SF	MLB	29	237	29	9	0	9	32	14	38	0	1	.266/.316/.453

Comparables: Aaron Hill, Robinson Canó, Carlos Baerga

Before the five-year fever dream that saw the Giants win three championships, the history of the team in San Francisco had been one of the sadder stories in the majors: three Series appearances, three losses, each uniquely painful (Bobby Richardson, Scott Spiezio/Troy Glaus) and/or bizarre (the 1989 Loma Prieta earthquake). There was also that cursed 1993 season that saw the team win 103 games, only to miss out on the playoffs because "Western" Division rival Atlanta Braves won 104. We digress. Flores made his case to be a spiritual OG (Original Giant) during the season's final weekend, after his three-run, possible-playoff-clinching homer was swept into the dustbin of history by Trent Grisham's walk-off shot. Ah well. The Giants will be happy to have Flores back, for the second season of a two-year deal, to create happier memories in 2021.

YEAR	TEAM	LVL	AGE	PA	DRC+	BABIP	BRR	FRAA	WARP
2018	NYM	MLB	26	429	105	.269	-3.2	1B(83): -2.6, 2B(13): 0.1, 3B(10): -1.1	0.4
2019	ARI	MLB	27	285	117	.332	-0.2	2B(64): -5.4, 1B(16): 0.1	1.0
2020	SF	MLB	28	213	117	.272	-1.5	1B(14): 0.6, 2B(14): 1.2, 3B(3): -0.4	0.9
2021 FS	SF	MLB	29	600	110	.282	-0.6	2B 0, 3B -1	1.9
2021 DC	SF	MLB	29	237	110	.282	-0.3	2B 0, 3B 0	0.8

Wilmer Flores, continued

Batted Ball Distribution

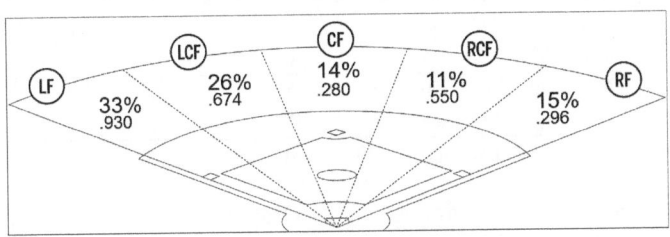

Strike Zone vs LHP   Strike Zone vs RHP

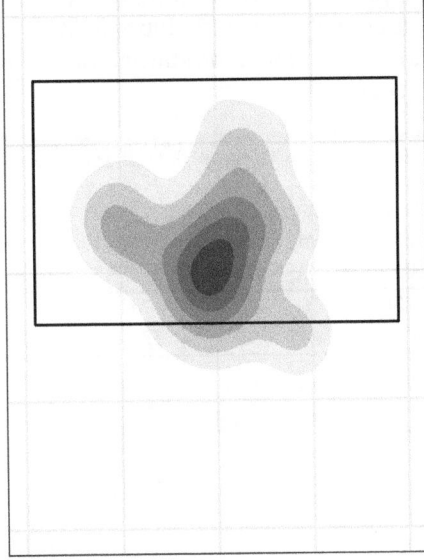

San Francisco Giants 2021

Tommy La Stella 2B
Born: 01/31/89 Age: 32 Bats: L Throws: R
Height: 5'11" Weight: 180 Origin: Round 8, 2011 Draft (#266 overall)

YEAR	TEAM	LVL	AGE	PA	R	2B	3B	HR	RBI	BB	K	SB	CS	AVG/OBP/SLG
2018	CHC	MLB	29	192	23	8	0	1	19	17	27	0	1	.266/.340/.331
2019	LAA	MLB	30	321	49	8	0	16	44	20	28	0	0	.295/.346/.486
2020	OAK	MLB	31	111	16	6	2	1	11	12	5	0	0	.289/.369/.423
2020	LAA	MLB	31	117	15	8	0	4	14	15	7	1	0	.273/.371/.475
2021 FS	SF	MLB	32	600	80	28	2	15	65	58	69	1	1	.273/.351/.423
2021 DC	SF	MLB	32	571	76	27	1	15	62	55	66	1	1	.273/.351/.423

Comparables: Davey Johnson, Mark Loretta, Glenn Hubbard

Last winter, people were saying it in whispers: "Tommy La Stella is … come closer … *good*." It seemed like a prank, a joke as cruel as La Stella being selected to his first All-Star team in the midst of a storybook 2019 season and almost immediately fracturing his right tibia via foul ball. When this season finally arrived, though, La Stella was just as good as in his first season with the Angels, and continued producing after being traded upstate to Oakland. The 30-home run pace didn't recur (frankly, if you expected it to, that's on you), but La Stella was actually the better hitter in 2020, proving the only joke was on the Cubs for never getting him the starting role he found in the AL West and rode into free agency.

YEAR	TEAM	LVL	AGE	PA	DRC+	BABIP	BRR	FRAA	WARP
2018	CHC	MLB	29	192	84	.312	0.7	3B(26): -1.8, 2B(15): 0.3, P(1): -0.0	0.2
2019	LAA	MLB	30	321	119	.282	-1.0	2B(46): -1.8, 3B(30): -1.1, 1B(3): -0.0	1.5
2020	OAK	MLB	31	111	124	.293	0.5	2B(18): 0.9, 3B(6): -0.2	0.7
2020	LAA	MLB	31	117	124	.258	-1.5	2B(15): -3.2, 1B(10): 0.0	0.1
2021 FS	SF	MLB	32	600	117	.288	-0.8	2B -3, 3B -1	2.3
2021 DC	SF	MLB	32	571	117	.288	-0.7	2B -3, 3B -1	2.3

Tommy La Stella, continued

Batted Ball Distribution

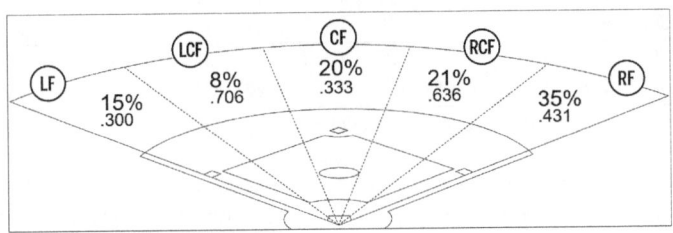

Strike Zone vs LHP

Strike Zone vs RHP

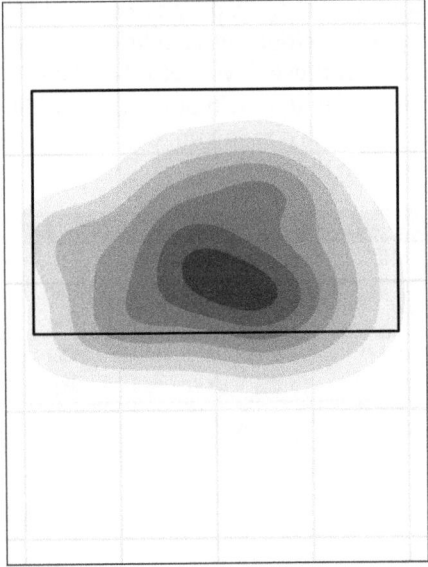

Evan Longoria 3B

Born: 10/07/85   Age: 35   Bats: R   Throws: R
Height: 6'1"   Weight: 213   Origin: Round 1, 2006 Draft (#3 overall)

YEAR	TEAM	LVL	AGE	PA	R	2B	3B	HR	RBI	BB	K	SB	CS	AVG/OBP/SLG
2018	SF	MLB	32	512	51	25	4	16	54	22	101	3	1	.244/.281/.412
2019	SF	MLB	33	508	59	19	2	20	69	43	112	3	1	.254/.325/.437
2020	SF	MLB	34	209	26	10	1	7	28	11	39	0	1	.254/.297/.425
2021 FS	SF	MLB	35	600	66	25	2	19	74	39	132	3	2	.236/.293/.400
2021 DC	SF	MLB	35	536	59	22	2	17	66	35	118	2	2	.236/.293/.400

Comparables: Ryan Zimmerman, Eric Chavez, Scott Rolen

If it seems like Longoria has been in San Francisco a lot longer than three years, it may be because he's been part of a narrative that the Giants have had to live with since the final days of the Sabean/Evans era: too many older, expensive players locked up for the long term. In addition to Longo, there's Belt, Crawford, Cueto and (even though it be blasphemy) Posey. When you press on that plotline, you see that Longoria has not been a complete disaster, and in fact has been roughly the same offensive player since his final year in Tampa Bay. But the other side of "not a complete disaster" is "slightly below league-average corner infielder, with declining defensive skills." It's not a profile that's much in demand these days. Batted-ball metrics from 2020 suggest that Longoria had a late-career uptick in power; it would be immensely helpful if he could pair this thump with a modicum of patience, lest Zaidi, Kapler and company begin to run short on theirs.

YEAR	TEAM	LVL	AGE	PA	DRC+	BABIP	BRR	FRAA	WARP
2018	SF	MLB	32	512	89	.274	-5.2	3B(123): -10.5	-0.5
2019	SF	MLB	33	508	99	.291	0.1	3B(119): 6.6	2.6
2020	SF	MLB	34	209	96	.280	-0.8	3B(52): -2.0	0.0
2021 FS	SF	MLB	35	600	89	.275	-0.3	3B -1	0.2
2021 DC	SF	MLB	35	536	89	.275	-0.3	3B -1	0.1

Evan Longoria, continued

Batted Ball Distribution

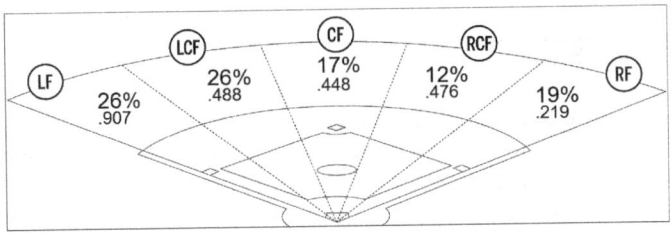

Strike Zone vs LHP

Strike Zone vs RHP

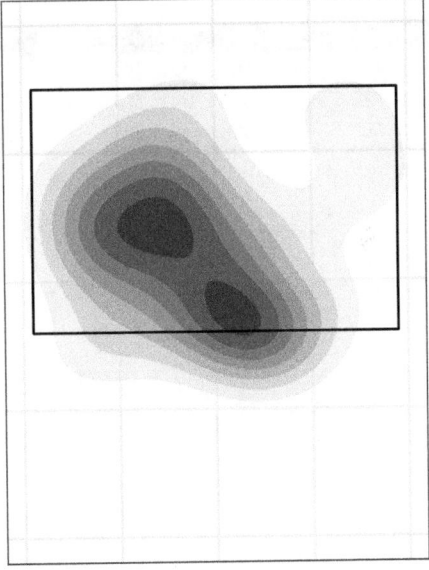

Darin Ruf 1B

Born: 07/28/86 Age: 34 Bats: R Throws: R
Height: 6'2" Weight: 232 Origin: Round 20, 2009 Draft (#617 overall)

YEAR	TEAM	LVL	AGE	PA	R	2B	3B	HR	RBI	BB	K	SB	CS	AVG/OBP/SLG
2020	SF	MLB	33	100	11	6	0	5	18	13	23	1	0	.276/.370/.517
2021 FS	SF	MLB	34	600	70	22	1	14	75	49	162	1	1	.219/.293/.347
2021 DC	SF	MLB	34	298	35	11	0	7	37	24	80	0	1	.219/.293/.347

Comparables: Brian Daubach, Tony Clark, Wil Myers

You better believe the 2020 Vogelsong Award winner gets the full-comment treatment here. After three years as a Samsung Lion, Ruf returned to American shores looking much more like the middle-of-the-order producer he showed in the KBO than the one-dimensional power bat who washed out with the Phillies. While in Korea, he added patience and worked on hitting to all fields, elevating him above a short-side platoon slot for the time being. To be fair, his role was greatly enhanced by the NL use of the DH in 2020, but the bat seemed to argue a case that, even at 34 and likely ticketed for a bench role, Ruf may have a surprisingly smooth second MLB act.

YEAR	TEAM	LVL	AGE	PA	DRC+	BABIP	BRR	FRAA	WARP
2020	SF	MLB	33	100	115	.322	-0.4	LF(22): 1.2, 1B(4): 0.1, RF(3): -0.4	0.4
2021 FS	SF	MLB	34	600	77	.283	-0.7	LF 8, 1B 0	0.4
2021 DC	SF	MLB	34	298	77	.283	-0.3	LF 4	0.1

Darin Ruf, continued

Batted Ball Distribution

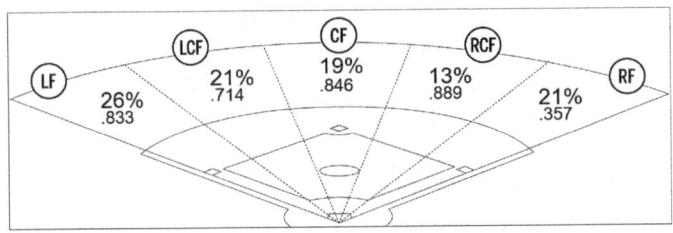

Strike Zone vs LHP   **Strike Zone vs RHP**

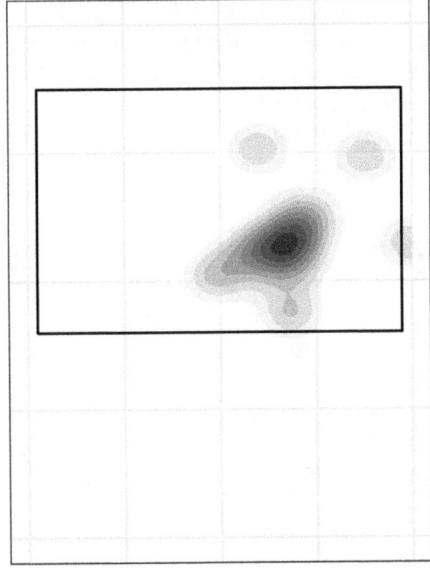

San Francisco Giants 2021

Austin Slater LF

Born: 12/13/92 Age: 28 Bats: R Throws: R
Height: 6'1" Weight: 204 Origin: Round 8, 2014 Draft (#238 overall)

YEAR	TEAM	LVL	AGE	PA	R	2B	3B	HR	RBI	BB	K	SB	CS	AVG/OBP/SLG
2018	SAC	AAA	25	223	32	24	2	5	32	21	39	8	2	.344/.417/.564
2018	SF	MLB	25	225	21	6	1	1	23	20	69	7	0	.251/.333/.307
2019	SAC	AAA	26	296	47	17	0	12	45	46	69	6	2	.308/.436/.529
2019	SF	MLB	26	192	20	9	3	5	21	22	59	1	0	.238/.333/.417
2020	SF	MLB	27	104	18	2	1	5	7	16	22	8	1	.282/.408/.506
2021 FS	SF	MLB	28	600	81	19	3	19	61	63	160	2	2	.243/.334/.402
2021 DC	SF	MLB	28	177	23	5	0	5	18	18	47	0	1	.243/.334/.402

Comparables: Jason Repko, Michael Restovich, Byron Browne

Last year's 60-game season already created an artificially small statistical snapshot; capturing the essence of Slater's impressive 2020 requires us to pare down the sample even smaller, to the season's first month. After August, Slater went from being sidelined with a right elbow flexor strain to being used only as a DH—a predicament that left him far less effective. But gosh, what a month August was, with Slater teeing off on the (mostly southpaw) arms of the Western, uh…Conference. He got there by upping both launch angle and walk rate, suggesting there's more a Quad-A ceiling to his bat. Unlike a previous generation's namesake, this Slater will likely be saved not by the bell but, rather, by playing the platoon wingman to a strong-sided Zack Morris type. So long as he keeps feasting on southpaws like they're a heaping of french fries at The Max, he should be able to avoid having his career screech to a halt.

YEAR	TEAM	LVL	AGE	PA	DRC+	BABIP	BRR	FRAA	WARP
2018	SAC	AAA	25	223	163	.405	1.4	RF(29): 0.6, 1B(13): -0.1, LF(6): -0.9	1.8
2018	SF	MLB	25	225	63	.377	1.3	LF(25): 1.8, 1B(21): 0.1, RF(14): -0.3	-0.2
2019	SAC	AAA	26	296	139	.388	0.6	1B(38): 2.5, 3B(11): -1.4, LF(8): -0.6	2.1
2019	SF	MLB	26	192	73	.337	-0.7	RF(46): -0.2, 1B(8): -0.8, LF(2): -0.1	-0.4
2020	SF	MLB	27	104	117	.328	0.4	RF(9): 1.5, LF(3): 0.4	0.6
2021 FS	SF	MLB	28	600	107	.311	-0.2	RF 2, 1B 0	1.9
2021 DC	SF	MLB	28	177	107	.311	-0.1	RF 1	0.5

Austin Slater, continued

Batted Ball Distribution

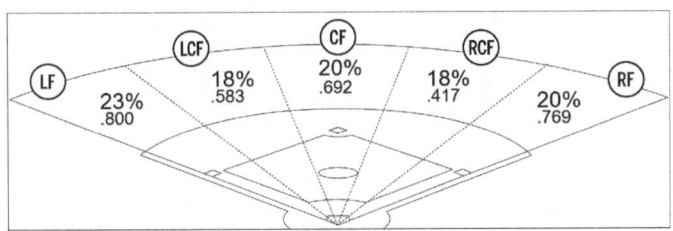

Strike Zone vs LHP   Strike Zone vs RHP

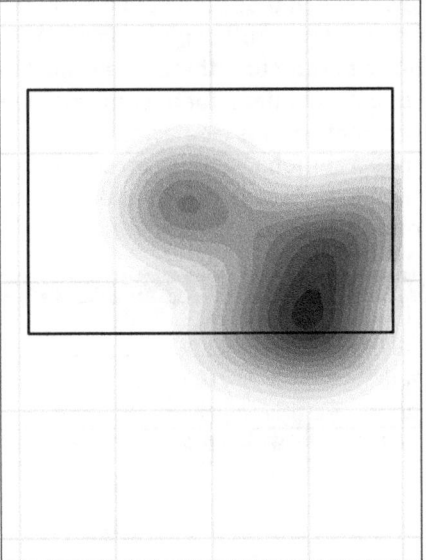

Justin Smoak 1B

Born: 12/05/86 Age: 34 Bats: S Throws: L
Height: 6'4" Weight: 220 Origin: Round 1, 2008 Draft (#11 overall)

YEAR	TEAM	LVL	AGE	PA	R	2B	3B	HR	RBI	BB	K	SB	CS	AVG/OBP/SLG
2018	TOR	MLB	31	594	67	34	0	25	77	83	155	0	1	.242/.350/.457
2019	TOR	MLB	32	500	54	16	0	22	61	79	106	0	0	.208/.342/.406
2020	SF	MLB	33	6	0	0	0	0	0	0	2	0	0	.000/.000/.000
2020	MIL	MLB	33	126	14	7	0	5	15	10	40	0	0	.186/.262/.381
2021 FS	SF	MLB	34	600	66	20	1	21	70	70	182	0	1	.206/.304/.375

Comparables: Paul Sorrento, Mark Johnson, John Jaha

By any measure, the top of the first round in the 2008 amateur draft was thick with high-impact college bats: Pedro Alvarez, Gordon Beckham, Yonder Alonso and of course, Buster Posey. Smoak was well in the conversation to be the best of these, and yet for all of his career longevity, the switch-hitter out of South Carolina has eked out a decade-long career that hasn't even tallied four wins—what we'd call a "meh" year for a healthy Posey. It all never really gelled for more than short stretches: the patience was there but the contact wasn't; the power showed but the patience couldn't hold; all the while, offspeed pitches remained the stuff of nightmares. A dismal start to 2020 with the Brewers, and then a perfunctory three-game spell with the Giants before his release, leaves his comment here, for a team you may not even know he'd joined. If this comment sounds elegiac, take heart from the fact that Smoak is not too old to ignite a comeback, if he can convince a team that there's still some glow in the embers. He'll seek to rekindle the flame with a new set of Giants, those of Yomiuri, in 2021.

YEAR	TEAM	LVL	AGE	PA	DRC+	BABIP	BRR	FRAA	WARP
2018	TOR	MLB	31	594	117	.296	-5.1	1B(134): -7.2	0.8
2019	TOR	MLB	32	500	110	.223	-2.0	1B(89): -5.5	0.7
2020	SF	MLB	33	6	76	.000			0.0
2020	MIL	MLB	33	126	78	.232	-1.1	1B(31): -4.0	-0.8
2021 FS	SF	MLB	34	600	90	.267	-0.9	1B -4	-0.4

Justin Smoak, continued

Batted Ball Distribution

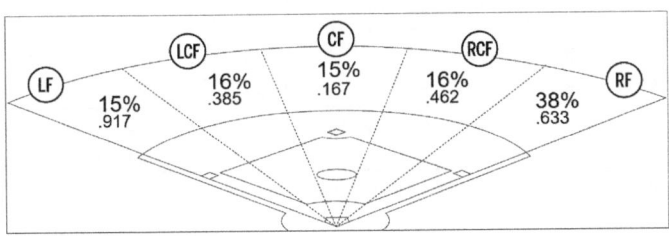

Strike Zone vs LHP   **Strike Zone vs RHP**

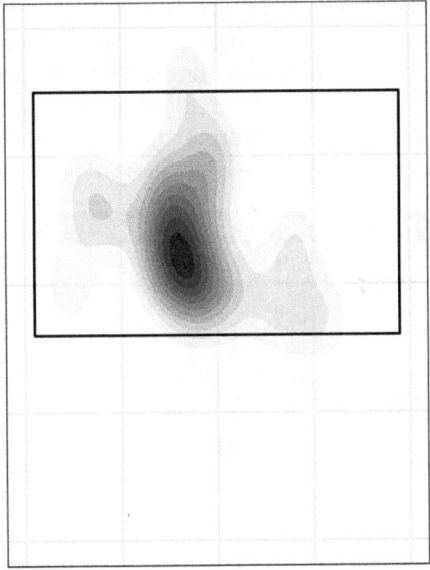

Donovan Solano SS

Born: 12/17/87 Age: 33 Bats: R Throws: R
Height: 5'8" Weight: 210 Origin: International Free Agent, 2005

YEAR	TEAM	LVL	AGE	PA	R	2B	3B	HR	RBI	BB	K	SB	CS	AVG/OBP/SLG
2018	DOD2	ROK	30	27	3	1	0	0	3	0	1	0	0	.440/.444/.480
2018	OKC	AAA	30	340	38	21	1	4	43	16	40	4	1	.318/.353/.430
2019	SAC	AAA	31	97	12	4	0	2	16	9	11	0	0	.322/.392/.437
2019	SF	MLB	31	228	27	13	1	4	23	10	49	0	1	.330/.360/.456
2020	SF	MLB	32	203	22	15	1	3	29	10	39	0	0	.326/.365/.463
2021 FS	SF	MLB	33	600	66	25	2	11	65	28	128	0	1	.260/.302/.376
2021 DC	SF	MLB	33	483	53	20	1	9	52	23	103	0	1	.260/.302/.376

Comparables: Terry Shumpert, Dick Green, Randy Velarde

There's no shortage of killjoys out there who will "well, actually" you when you refer to Solano by his newly-minted "Donnie Barrels" nickname. The fact that his barrel percentage is *only* in the 21st percentile shouldn't dampen the rest of Solano's two-season breakout as a legitimately good hitter after what seemed like a short (and pretty much finished) career as a utility infielder. While the smart money is on regression to something less than the sixth-best batting average in the majors, Solano 2.0 seems plenty capable of spraying line drives around the park, whatever Statcast pedants may call them. Heading into his final arb year at the advanced age of 33, the current Giants front office approaches personnel decisions with a Raysian unsentimentality, so even a catchy nickname is no guarantee of an everyday role in 2021.

YEAR	TEAM	LVL	AGE	PA	DRC+	BABIP	BRR	FRAA	WARP
2018	DOD2	ROK	30	27		.440			
2018	OKC	AAA	30	340	107	.348	-1.2	SS(65): -1.9, 2B(10): 0.7, 3B(4): 0.5	1.1
2019	SAC	AAA	31	97	111	.351	-0.9	2B(14): 0.4, 3B(10): 0.3, SS(1): -0.0	0.5
2019	SF	MLB	31	228	100	.409	1.7	2B(36): -2.6, SS(19): 0.5, 3B(2): 0.0	0.9
2020	SF	MLB	32	203	109	.396	-1.6	2B(45): -4.3, 3B(5): -0.9, SS(2): -0.3	0.0
2021 FS	SF	MLB	33	600	87	.317	-0.8	2B -1, SS 0	0.5
2021 DC	SF	MLB	33	483	87	.317	-0.6	2B -1, SS 0	0.4

Donovan Solano, continued

Batted Ball Distribution

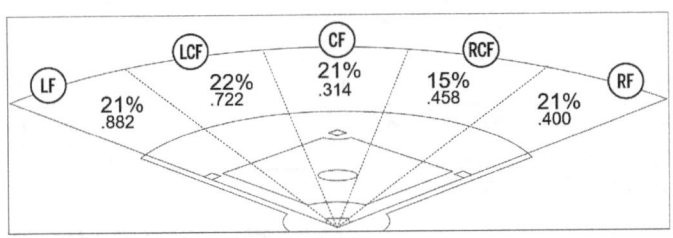

Strike Zone vs LHP   **Strike Zone vs RHP**

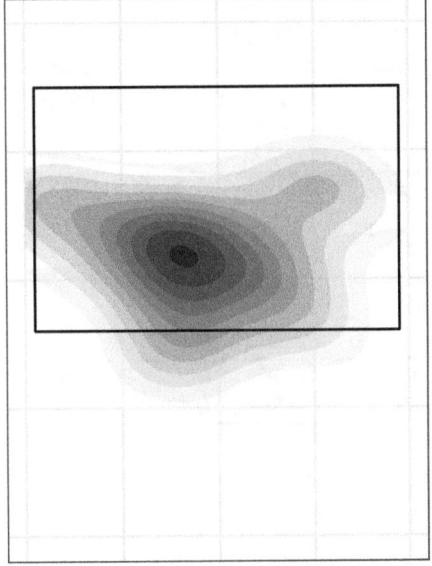

San Francisco Giants 2021

Chadwick Tromp C
Born: 03/21/95   Age: 26   Bats: R   Throws: R
Height: 5'8"   Weight: 221   Origin: International Free Agent, 2013

YEAR	TEAM	LVL	AGE	PA	R	2B	3B	HR	RBI	BB	K	SB	CS	AVG/OBP/SLG
2018	PNS	AA	23	98	9	5	0	0	10	12	18	0	1	.247/.340/.306
2018	LOU	AAA	23	195	20	8	1	2	14	15	24	2	2	.264/.333/.356
2019	RED	ROK	24	61	10	5	0	2	16	11	10	0	0	.271/.410/.500
2019	LOU	AAA	24	90	15	2	1	7	21	11	25	0	1	.286/.389/.610
2020	SF	MLB	25	64	11	1	0	4	10	1	20	0	0	.213/.219/.426
2021 FS	SF	MLB	26	600	65	22	2	15	62	45	161	0	1	.215/.282/.350
2021 DC	SF	MLB	26	61	6	2	0	1	6	4	16	0	0	.215/.282/.350

Comparables: J.R. Towles, Rob Bowen, Jason Jaramillo

While Tromp possesses an 80-grade name (with a similarly excellent spoonerism), his baseball-related skill set is considerably less exceptional. Still, a power bat and capable defense is the minimum requirement for a backup job in the bigs, and a memeable name is an added benefit for a team's social media coordinator, if not the team itself.

YEAR	TEAM	P. COUNT	FRM RUNS	BLK RUNS	THRW RUNS	TOT RUNS
2018	LOU	6895	1.8	0.1	1.1	3.0
2018	PNS	3305	3.4	0.3	-0.1	3.5
2019	LOU	3028	-1.8	0.0	-0.4	-2.3
2020	SF	2756	2.0	-0.1	0.0	1.9
2021	SF	2405	1.9	0.0	0.1	2.0
2021	SF	2405	1.9	0.2	0.1	2.1

YEAR	TEAM	LVL	AGE	PA	DRC+	BABIP	BRR	FRAA	WARP
2018	PNS	AA	23	98	102	.313	-0.4	C(25): 3.7	0.7
2018	LOU	AAA	23	195	102	.293	-2.2	C(51): 1.8	0.7
2019	RED	ROK	24	61		.297			
2019	LOU	AAA	24	90	125	.333	0.5	C(22): -2.2	0.5
2020	SF	MLB	25	64	81	.231	0.2	C(23): -0.1	0.4
2021 FS	SF	MLB	26	600	75	.273	-0.7	C 14	2.0
2021 DC	SF	MLB	26	61	75	.273	-0.1	C 2	0.3

Chadwick Tromp, continued

Batted Ball Distribution

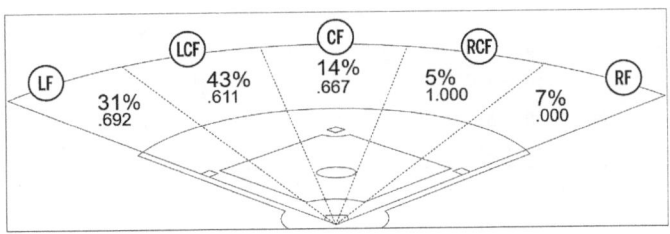

Strike Zone vs LHP   Strike Zone vs RHP

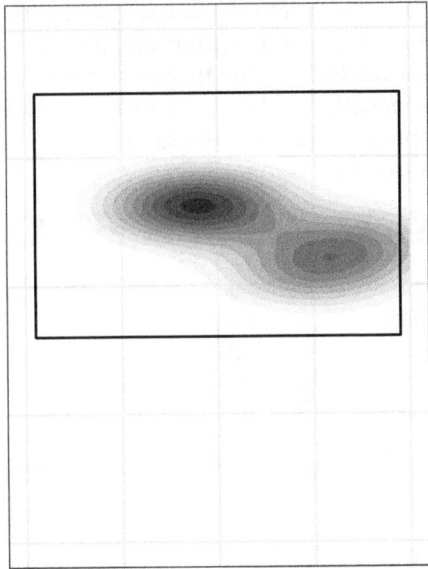

Mike Yastrzemski LF

Born: 08/23/90   Age: 30   Bats: L   Throws: L
Height: 5'10"   Weight: 178   Origin: Round 14, 2013 Draft (#429 overall)

YEAR	TEAM	LVL	AGE	PA	R	2B	3B	HR	RBI	BB	K	SB	CS	AVG/OBP/SLG
2018	BOW	AA	27	117	13	10	0	1	11	10	30	2	1	.202/.276/.327
2018	NOR	AAA	27	374	48	18	6	9	49	44	75	6	4	.265/.359/.441
2019	SAC	AAA	28	163	38	11	1	12	25	22	36	2	2	.316/.414/.676
2019	SF	MLB	28	411	64	22	3	21	55	32	107	2	4	.272/.334/.518
2020	SF	MLB	29	225	39	14	4	10	35	30	55	2	1	.297/.400/.568
2021 FS	SF	MLB	30	600	87	27	6	22	70	61	161	2	1	.246/.331/.452
2021 DC	SF	MLB	30	618	89	28	6	23	72	63	166	2	1	.246/.331/.452

Comparables: Reggie Sanders, Brad Hawpe, Jesse Barfield

It was a great story in 2019—Hall of Famer's grandson who worked hard through the minors, made it to the bigs with a rebuilding team and even hit a home run in Fenway Park of all places!—and here we were, ready for the closing credits of the inspirational baseball film. But then Yaz produced a sequel that few expected: improved plate discipline, excellent quality of contact, defense good enough to play a passable center field, all the while inspiring sputtering mea culpas from writers and analysts all-too-ready to dismiss the late bloomer. We walked into the theater thinking we were getting a warmed-over *Rudy* knockoff, and Yaz gave us *The Thirty-Year-Old MVP Candidate*. Even if the next episode is more of the same, it'll be the kind of fan service that will disappoint absolutely no one.

YEAR	TEAM	LVL	AGE	PA	DRC+	BABIP	BRR	FRAA	WARP
2018	BOW	AA	27	117	76	.270	1.5	LF(14): 0.9, RF(7): 1.5, CF(4): -0.1	0.2
2018	NOR	AAA	27	374	129	.320	4.3	LF(50): 8.7, CF(36): 2.2, RF(8): 2.3	3.5
2019	SAC	AAA	28	163	145	.344	2.2	CF(21): -0.2, LF(8): -0.3, RF(7): 0.4	1.6
2019	SF	MLB	28	411	111	.325	0.5	LF(61): -0.5, RF(56): 0.3, CF(7): -0.3	1.7
2020	SF	MLB	29	225	123	.370	-0.2	RF(31): 3.4, CF(24): 1.4, LF(8): 0.2	1.7
2021 FS	SF	MLB	30	600	117	.309	0.0	RF 6, CF 0	3.5
2021 DC	SF	MLB	30	618	117	.309	0.0	RF 6, CF 0	3.4

Mike Yastrzemski, continued

Batted Ball Distribution

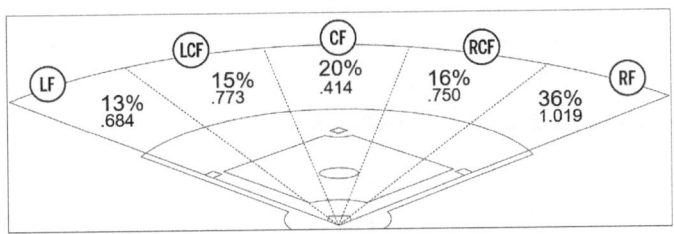

Strike Zone vs LHP   Strike Zone vs RHP

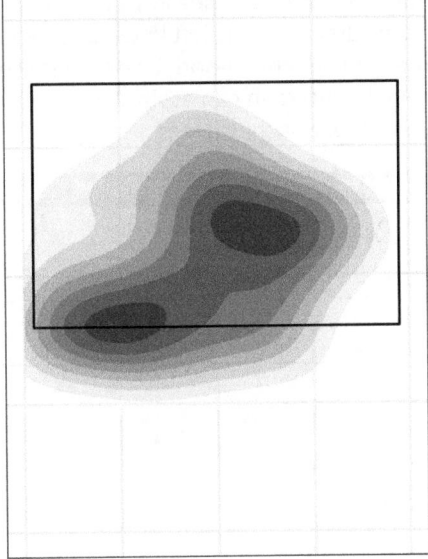

Tyler Anderson LHP

Born: 12/30/89 Age: 31 Bats: L Throws: L
Height: 6'2" Weight: 213 Origin: Round 1, 2011 Draft (#20 overall)

YEAR	TEAM	LVL	AGE	W	L	SV	G	GS	IP	H	HR	BB/9	K/9	K	GB%	BABIP
2018	COL	MLB	28	7	9	0	32	32	176	165	30	3.0	8.4	164	36.8%	.282
2019	COL	MLB	29	0	3	0	5	5	20²	33	8	4.8	10.0	23	38.9%	.403
2020	SF	MLB	30	4	3	0	13	11	59²	58	5	3.8	6.2	41	28.9%	.288
2021 FS	SF	MLB	31	9	8	0	26	26	150	150	24	3.1	7.5	125	35.4%	.291
2021 DC	SF	MLB	31	8	8	0	25	25	132	132	21	3.1	7.5	110	35.4%	.291

Comparables: Anthony DeSclafani, Sam Gaviglio, Brent Suter

    Anderson is yet another beneficiary of Farhan Zaidi's Emma Lazarus approach to player acquisition, through which he ardently collects the league's tired, poor, discarded, misdeveloped and/or post-injury players yearning to breathe free on a major-league roster. Among these huddled masses, Anderson in particular found the air much more comfortable at sea level than a mile above it. As a starter for the Rockies, the lefty showed just enough to make us feel bad that he was stuck in Colorado. After being picked up on waivers by the Giants, Anderson used the season's delayed commencement to fully work his way back from surgery on his left knee, and he emerged in 2020 as a starter more useful than consistently good. Under team control for another year, it remains to be seen if Anderson can assimilate into a Giants rotation that is certain to include a varied cast of characters.

YEAR	TEAM	LVL	AGE	WHIP	ERA	DRA-	WARP	MPH	FB%	WHF	CSP
2018	COL	MLB	28	1.27	4.55	107	1.0	93.9	44.5%	25.3%	
2019	COL	MLB	29	2.13	11.76	116	0.0	93.5	47.6%	24.2%	
2020	SF	MLB	30	1.39	4.37	144	-0.9	92.2	47.0%	24.6%	
2021 FS	SF	MLB	31	1.35	4.53	102	1.3	93.1	46.0%	24.9%	48.8%
2021 DC	SF	MLB	31	1.35	4.53	102	1.1	93.1	46.0%	24.9%	48.8%

Tyler Anderson, continued

Pitch Shape vs LHH

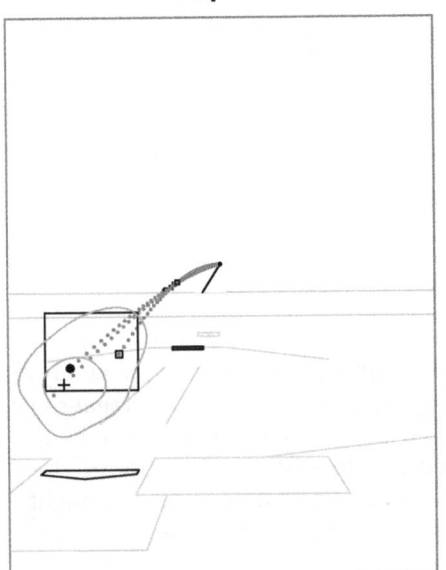

Pitch Shape vs RHH

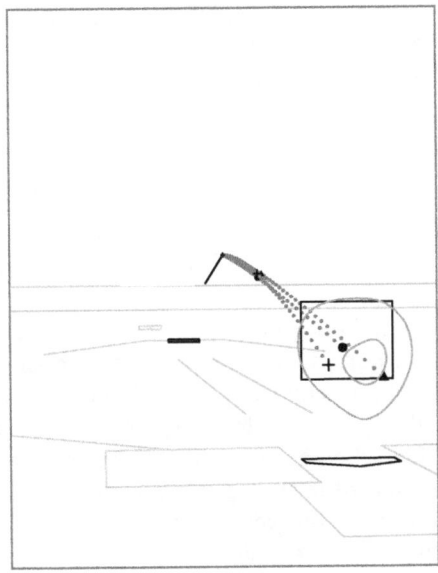

Type	Frequency	Velocity	H Movement	V Movement
● Fastball	38.3%	90.3 [93]	6.9 [99]	-12.9 [106]
□ Sinker	8.7%	89.5 [85]	12.4 [105]	-18.5 [107]
+ Cutter	18.1%	85 [79]	-2.9 [106]	-25.1 [96]
▲ Changeup	33.0%	80.9 [83]	10.1 [108]	-24.2 [109]

Caleb Baragar LHP

Born: 04/09/94 Age: 27 Bats: R Throws: L
Height: 6'3" Weight: 215 Origin: Round 9, 2016 Draft (#275 overall)

YEAR	TEAM	LVL	AGE	W	L	SV	G	GS	IP	H	HR	BB/9	K/9	K	GB%	BABIP
2018	AUG	LO-A	24	2	2	0	16	11	67	62	9	1.7	9.8	73	23.6%	.321
2018	SJ	HI-A	24	1	2	0	8	1	11^1	13	0	4.8	9.5	12	47.4%	.342
2018	SAC	AAA	24	0	0	0	2	0	3^2	3	1	0.0	0.0	0	14.3%	.154
2019	SJ	HI-A	25	0	1	0	5	4	16^2	15	2	4.3	11.9	22	35.7%	.333
2019	RIC	AA	25	5	5	0	22	21	120	83	12	3.2	8.0	107	28.4%	.225
2019	SAC	AAA	25	0	0	0	1	1	4^1	6	1	4.2	12.5	6	33.3%	.455
2020	SF	MLB	26	5	1	0	24	1	22^1	17	3	2.0	7.7	19	20.6%	.233
2021 FS	SF	MLB	27	2	3	0	57	0	50	49	10	3.5	8.2	45	28.6%	.279
2021 DC	SF	MLB	27	2	2	0	51	0	45.3	44	9	3.5	8.2	41	28.6%	.279

Comparables: Ben Braymer, Aaron Sanchez, Joe Ross

Kill the win? Baragar would like to adopt the win, give it its own en suite bedroom, swaddle it in sheets of obscenely high thread count, buy it a pony and start up a college fund for it. Although only logging 22 ⅓ innings, Baragar's five W's equaled the total of some hurlers you'll probably recognize: Aaron Nola, Max Scherzer, Trevor Bauer, Tyler Glasnow and José Berríos, for starters. The bad news for Baragar (and any potential win-based arbitration case he might make in a few years) is that his profile—a high-spin, mid-90s four-seamer, and little else—sets him up for a short relief role. He's more likely to have a season with five saves than five wins (with either outcome an extreme longshot), but he'll always have 2020 on the back of his baseball card.

YEAR	TEAM	LVL	AGE	WHIP	ERA	DRA-	WARP	MPH	FB%	WHF	CSP
2018	AUG	LO-A	24	1.12	4.03	80	1.0				
2018	SJ	HI-A	24	1.68	4.76	66	0.2				
2018	SAC	AAA	24	0.82	2.45	104	0.0				
2019	SJ	HI-A	25	1.38	2.70	71	0.3				
2019	RIC	AA	25	1.05	3.45	76	1.8				
2019	SAC	AAA	25	1.85	10.38	77	0.1				
2020	SF	MLB	26	0.99	4.03	126	-0.1	95.4	75.1%	19.1%	
2021 FS	SF	MLB	27	1.38	4.81	114	-0.2	95.4	75.1%	19.1%	53.8%
2021 DC	SF	MLB	27	1.38	4.81	114	-0.1	95.4	75.1%	19.1%	53.8%

Caleb Baragar, continued

Pitch Shape vs LHH

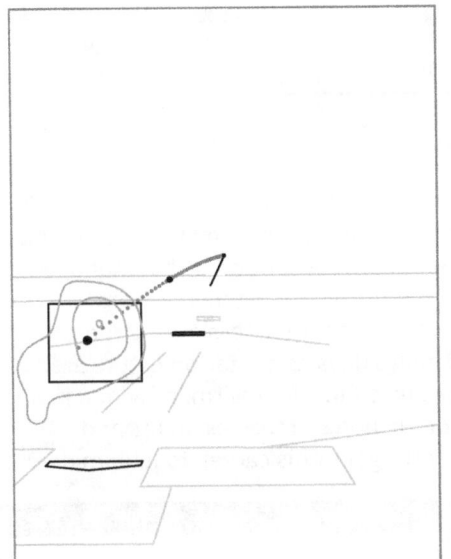

Pitch Shape vs RHH

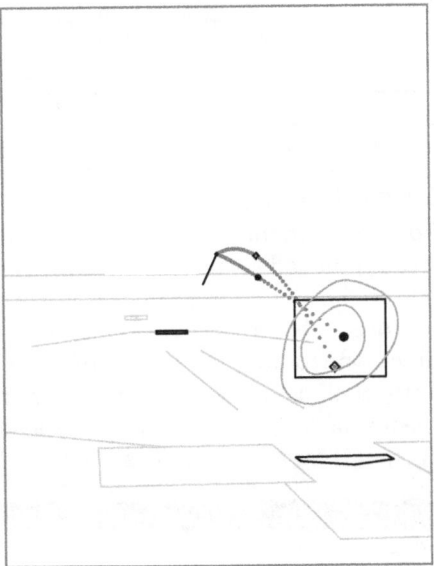

Type	Frequency	Velocity	H Movement	V Movement
● Fastball	75.1%	93.9 [104]	7.1 [98]	-10.9 [112]
▽ Slider	14.3%	83.9 [100]	-7.5 [108]	-35 [96]
◇ Curveball	10.3%	79.4 [103]	-11.8 [117]	-45.8 [106]

Trevor Cahill   RHP

Born: 03/01/88   Age: 33   Bats: R   Throws: R
Height: 6'4"   Weight: 223   Origin: Round 2, 2006 Draft (#66 overall)

YEAR	TEAM	LVL	AGE	W	L	SV	G	GS	IP	H	HR	BB/9	K/9	K	GB%	BABIP
2018	NAS	AAA	30	0	1	0	3	3	13^2	7	0	5.3	11.2	17	80.6%	.226
2018	OAK	MLB	30	7	4	0	21	20	110	90	8	3.4	8.2	100	51.5%	.281
2019	LAA	MLB	31	4	9	0	37	11	102^1	111	25	3.4	7.1	81	45.9%	.283
2020	SF	MLB	32	1	2	0	11	6	25	16	3	5.0	11.2	31	32.2%	.236
2021 FS	SF	MLB	33	2	2	0	57	0	50	45	6	4.3	9.3	51	45.7%	.288

Comparables: Jhoulys Chacín, Tom Gorzelanny, Ryan Dempster

If Cahill can somehow make the necessary sacrifices to keep the Injury Gods from his door, there may be a useful final act of his up-and-down career. He has steadily moved away from his sinker, an excellent turf-pounder that managed to outrun the launch angle episteme. He now features that pitch in a more balanced mix with a changeup and curve, a recipe for success during the good times, and for mere survival otherwise. Cahill's days as a rotation fixture are likely behind him, but there may be some life left in a relief arm, provided it, and the rest of him, can stay one step ahead of the bones, muscles, joints and ligaments that seem to have been fated, throughout his career, to let him down.

YEAR	TEAM	LVL	AGE	WHIP	ERA	DRA-	WARP	MPH	FB%	WHF	CSP
2018	NAS	AAA	30	1.10	2.63	37	0.6				
2018	OAK	MLB	30	1.19	3.76	77	2.3	93.8	41.1%	27.9%	
2019	LAA	MLB	31	1.47	5.98	122	-0.4	93.5	36.5%	24.2%	
2020	SF	MLB	32	1.20	3.24	89	0.4	92.3	35.5%	28.7%	
2021 FS	SF	MLB	33	1.38	4.09	98	0.3	93.3	37.5%	26.1%	45.7%

Trevor Cahill, continued

Pitch Shape vs LHH

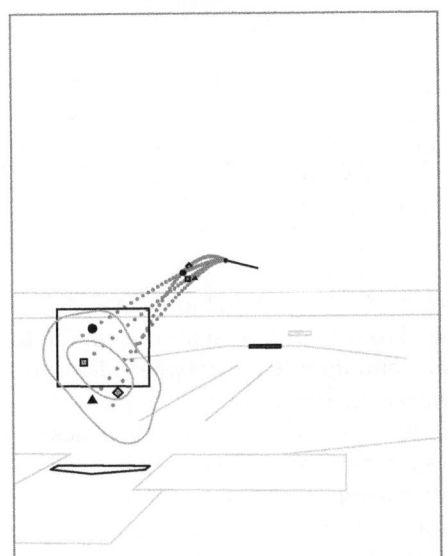

Pitch Shape vs RHH

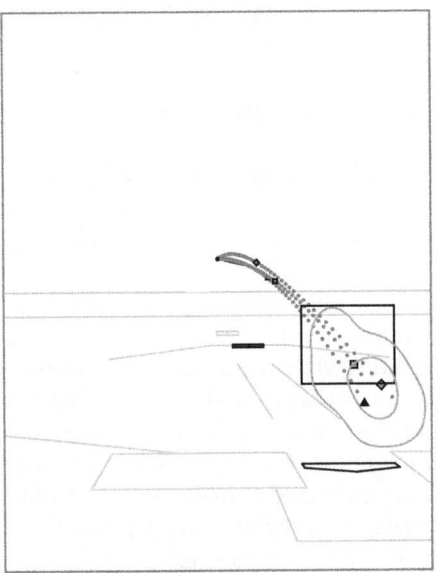

Type	Frequency	Velocity	H Movement	V Movement
● Fastball	8.8%	90.8 [94]	-7.1 [98]	-18.3 [91]
☐ Sinker	26.7%	90.8 [92]	-14.2 [92]	-23.5 [90]
▲ Changeup	29.1%	82.6 [90]	-12.1 [98]	-34.5 [81]
▽ Slider	12.4%	85.1 [105]	0.6 [83]	-31.7 [106]
◇ Curveball	23.0%	78.4 [99]	9.9 [110]	-50.8 [95]

Johnny Cueto RHP

Born: 02/15/86   Age: 35   Bats: R   Throws: R
Height: 5'11"   Weight: 229   Origin: International Free Agent, 2004

YEAR	TEAM	LVL	AGE	W	L	SV	G	GS	IP	H	HR	BB/9	K/9	K	GB%	BABIP
2018	SAC	AAA	32	0	0	0	2	2	7^2	5	0	1.2	11.7	10	38.9%	.278
2018	SF	MLB	32	3	2	0	9	9	53	46	8	2.2	6.5	38	42.4%	.259
2019	SJ	HI-A	33	0	1	0	2	2	7	8	1	1.3	6.4	5	52.2%	.333
2019	SAC	AAA	33	0	1	0	2	2	10^1	10	2	0.0	7.8	9	51.6%	.286
2019	SF	MLB	33	1	2	0	4	4	16	11	3	5.1	7.3	13	51.1%	.200
2020	SF	MLB	34	2	3	0	12	12	63^1	61	9	3.7	8.0	56	42.2%	.284
2021 FS	SF	MLB	35	9	8	0	26	26	150	145	21	3.0	7.7	128	43.2%	.284
2021 DC	SF	MLB	35	8	8	0	27	25	134.7	130	19	3.0	7.7	115	43.2%	.284

Comparables: Aníbal Sánchez, Jordan Zimmermann, Freddy Garcia

In an age of Driveline-inspired pitch design, PhD-powered biomechanical studies and the ruthless efficiencies applied to workouts, diet and sleep, Cueto is a throwback. His Instagram is a dizzying pendulum swing between absurdly decadent feasts and intensely penitent workouts, the latter reflecting an impressive strength and flexibility at odds with his highly relatable thiccness. On the mound, his motion is less a refined, repeatable mechanism for pitch delivery than a stylized performance resembling some minor form of modern dance, as he varies occasional quick pitches with comically baroque moves, at times freezing into statuesque poses for what feels like several seconds. There was a time when all of Cueto's flair was supported by skills and stamina that garnered him a couple of six-WARP seasons in the mid-2010s. Sadly, but inevitably, the skills have eroded, a demise perhaps accelerated by a Tommy John surgery that cost him nearly all of his 2019. Cueto remains a viable back-end starter—for now—but regardless of the declining career arc, he will stop, start, twist, turn, shimmy, herk and jerk against the dying of the light.

YEAR	TEAM	LVL	AGE	WHIP	ERA	DRA-	WARP	MPH	FB%	WHF	CSP
2018	SAC	AAA	32	0.78	0.00	77	0.2				
2018	SF	MLB	32	1.11	3.23	101	0.5	92.0	46.8%	21.8%	
2019	SJ	HI-A	33	1.29	6.43	117	-0.1				
2019	SAC	AAA	33	0.97	2.61	75	0.3				
2019	SF	MLB	33	1.25	5.06	90	0.2	93.0	51.3%	19.6%	
2020	SF	MLB	34	1.37	5.40	108	0.3	93.2	43.6%	19.9%	
2021 FS	SF	MLB	35	1.30	4.03	99	1.5	93.0	45.0%	20.2%	44.1%
2021 DC	SF	MLB	35	1.30	4.03	99	1.4	93.0	45.0%	20.2%	44.1%

Johnny Cueto, continued

Pitch Shape vs LHH

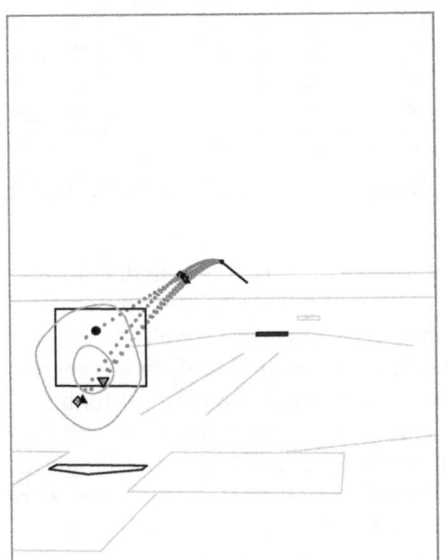

Pitch Shape vs RHH

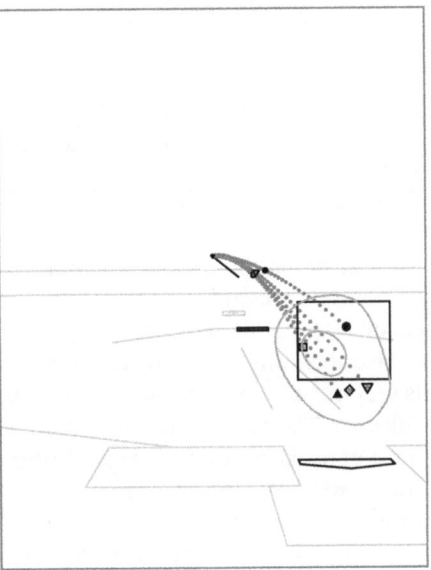

Type	Frequency	Velocity	H Movement	V Movement
● Fastball	30.5%	91.4 [96]	-9.3 [88]	-15.7 [99]
□ Sinker	13.0%	90.7 [91]	-14.2 [92]	-21.2 [98]
▲ Changeup	26.9%	82.4 [89]	-10 [109]	-31.9 [88]
▽ Slider	15.8%	83.5 [98]	1.9 [87]	-30.3 [110]
◇ Curveball	13.5%	79.8 [105]	3.1 [82]	-39 [121]

San Francisco Giants 2021

Anthony DeSclafani   RHP
Born: 04/18/90   Age: 31   Bats: R   Throws: R
Height: 6'2"   Weight: 195   Origin: Round 6, 2011 Draft (#199 overall)

YEAR	TEAM	LVL	AGE	W	L	SV	G	GS	IP	H	HR	BB/9	K/9	K	GB%	BABIP
2018	PNS	AA	28	0	1	0	2	2	8	5	0	1.1	13.5	12	58.8%	.294
2018	LOU	AAA	28	0	2	0	2	2	11^1	15	5	1.6	7.9	10	43.2%	.312
2018	CIN	MLB	28	7	8	0	21	21	115	118	24	2.3	8.5	108	40.7%	.298
2019	CIN	MLB	29	9	9	0	31	31	166^2	151	29	2.6	9.0	167	42.0%	.276
2020	CIN	MLB	30	1	2	0	9	7	33^2	41	7	4.3	6.7	25	39.5%	.318
2021 FS	SF	MLB	31	9	8	0	26	26	150	145	21	2.9	8.0	133	41.5%	.288
2021 DC	SF	MLB	31	7	6	0	25	22	108.7	105	15	2.9	8.0	96	41.5%	.288

Comparables: Jake Odorizzi, Nathan Eovaldi, Shaun Marcum

The 2020 highlights for DeSclafani were the August birth of his first child, a son named Cru, and the 11 scoreless innings the dad-to-be twirled to start the season. The lowlights were every outing after that, as Disco Demolition Night broke out whenever the New Jersey native took the mound. DeSclafani pitched his way out of the rotation and off the post-season roster, a bad result for his walk year. The sore shoulder that plagued him at the beginning of the year may have been a contributing factor, but the most likely culprit is also the simplest: poor fastball command. His velocity and the shape of his breaking pitches were normal, but he repeatedly missed his spots, walked the yard and served up more meatballs than a deli counter at lunch rush. DeSclafani has always been prone to the long ball and his stuff is never overpowering enough to play on its own, but when he's healthy and precise he can survive at the back end of the rotation. He'll try to be both of those things with San Francisco, inking a one-year, $6 million pact over the winter.

YEAR	TEAM	LVL	AGE	WHIP	ERA	DRA-	WARP	MPH	FB%	WHF	CSP
2018	PNS	AA	28	0.75	2.25	93	0.1				
2018	LOU	AAA	28	1.50	6.35	124	-0.1				
2018	CIN	MLB	28	1.29	4.93	115	0.2	95.5	57.9%	23.0%	
2019	CIN	MLB	29	1.20	3.89	80	3.3	96.2	55.4%	23.5%	
2020	CIN	MLB	30	1.69	7.22	137	-0.4	96.6	51.3%	23.2%	
2021 FS	SF	MLB	31	1.30	3.92	97	1.7	96.2	55.0%	23.3%	46.0%
2021 DC	SF	MLB	31	1.30	3.92	97	1.2	96.2	55.0%	23.3%	46.0%

Anthony DeSclafani, continued

Pitch Shape vs LHH

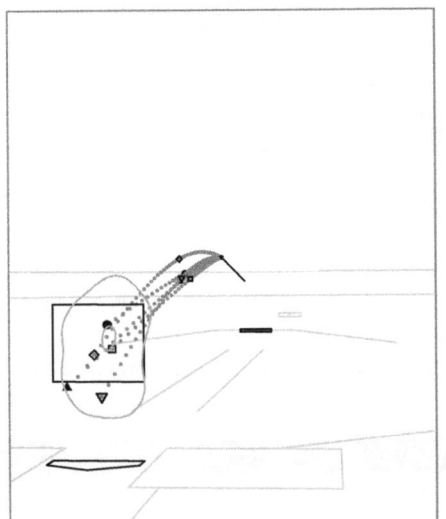

Pitch Shape vs RHH

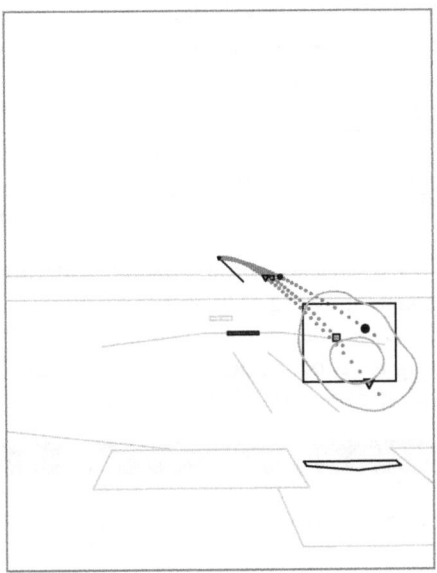

Type	Frequency	Velocity	H Movement	V Movement
● Fastball	33.1%	95.1 [108]	-7.2 [98]	-12.7 [107]
□ Sinker	18.3%	95 [113]	-12.4 [105]	-16.7 [112]
▲ Changeup	7.0%	88.6 [114]	-13.1 [93]	-25.9 [104]
▽ Slider	32.1%	86.4 [111]	3.7 [94]	-33.9 [100]
◇ Curveball	9.6%	82 [113]	6.3 [95]	-43.4 [111]

Jarlín García LHP

Born: 01/18/93   Age: 28   Bats: L   Throws: L
Height: 6'3"   Weight: 215   Origin: International Free Agent, 2010

YEAR	TEAM	LVL	AGE	W	L	SV	G	GS	IP	H	HR	BB/9	K/9	K	GB%	BABIP
2018	NO	AAA	25	2	2	0	10	9	48²	57	5	2.6	6.1	33	38.0%	.323
2018	MIA	MLB	25	3	3	0	29	7	66	59	16	3.8	5.5	40	43.3%	.223
2019	NO	AAA	26	2	0	0	7	0	9¹	6	1	3.9	10.6	11	38.1%	.250
2019	MIA	MLB	26	4	2	0	53	0	50²	40	4	2.8	6.9	39	46.3%	.250
2020	SF	MLB	27	2	1	0	19	0	18¹	11	0	3.4	6.9	14	46.0%	.220
2021 FS	SF	MLB	28	2	3	0	57	0	50	49	7	3.9	8.0	44	43.2%	.291
2021 DC	SF	MLB	28	6	3	0	49	3	55	54	8	3.9	8.0	48	43.2%	.291

Comparables: John Gant, Michael Feliz, Austin Brice

  Formerly known as Jarlin the Marlin, García the Giant took well to the other coast, allowing only one earned run over the course of the season. His contact-heavy profile suggests that his ERA will inevitably float upriver, at which point he might be forced downstream to Anaheim, where he could leverage his middle name to become Emmanuel the Angel.

YEAR	TEAM	LVL	AGE	WHIP	ERA	DRA-	WARP	MPH	FB%	WHF	CSP
2018	NO	AAA	25	1.46	4.81	86	0.8				
2018	MIA	MLB	25	1.32	4.91	123	-0.3	93.9	52.1%	19.3%	
2019	NO	AAA	26	1.07	1.93	68	0.3				
2019	MIA	MLB	26	1.11	3.02	80	0.8	94.8	39.8%	20.9%	
2020	SF	MLB	27	0.98	0.49	94	0.2	95.2	48.6%	15.8%	
2021 FS	SF	MLB	28	1.42	4.45	105	0.1	94.6	45.7%	19.1%	52.2%
2021 DC	SF	MLB	28	1.42	4.45	105	0.1	94.6	45.7%	19.1%	52.2%

Jarlín García, continued

Pitch Shape vs LHH	Pitch Shape vs RHH
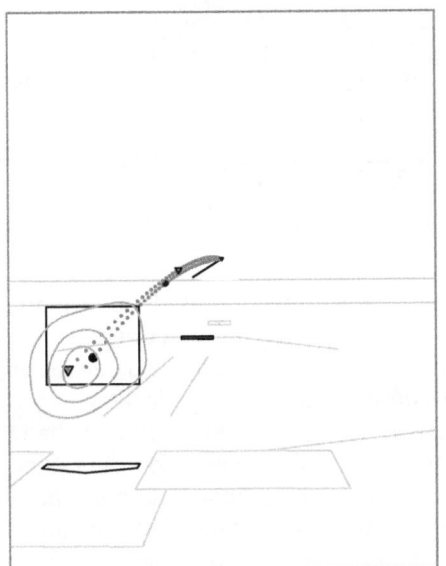	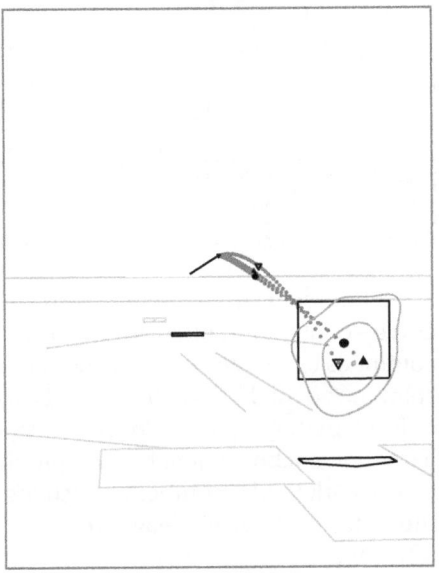

Type	Frequency	Velocity	H Movement	V Movement
● Fastball	47.6%	93.7 [104]	13.8 [66]	-17.5 [93]
▲ Changeup	17.9%	85.9 [103]	15.3 [81]	-26.6 [102]
▽ Slider	32.4%	83.5 [98]	-5.8 [102]	-34.8 [97]

Kevin Gausman RHP

Born: 01/06/91   Age: 30   Bats: L   Throws: R
Height: 6'2"   Weight: 190   Origin: Round 1, 2012 Draft (#4 overall)

YEAR	TEAM	LVL	AGE	W	L	SV	G	GS	IP	H	HR	BB/9	K/9	K	GB%	BABIP
2018	BAL	MLB	27	5	8	0	21	21	124	139	21	2.3	7.5	104	47.8%	.317
2018	ATL	MLB	27	5	3	0	10	10	59²	50	5	2.7	6.6	44	42.7%	.260
2019	GWN	AAA	28	0	1	0	1	1	7	6	1	1.3	12.9	10	62.5%	.357
2019	ATL	MLB	28	3	7	0	16	16	80	92	12	3.0	9.6	85	36.1%	.354
2019	CIN	MLB	28	0	2	0	15	1	22¹	21	3	2.0	11.7	29	41.1%	.346
2020	SF	MLB	29	3	3	0	12	10	59²	50	8	2.4	11.9	79	40.7%	.298
2021 FS	SF	MLB	30	10	7	0	26	26	150	132	20	3.1	10.2	170	41.9%	.293
2021 DC	SF	MLB	30	10	8	0	27	27	148.7	131	19	3.1	10.2	169	41.9%	.293

Comparables: Anthony DeSclafani, Jake Odorizzi, Julio Teheran

If a Gaussian curve is a symmetrical, bell-shaped distribution, the Gausman curve—or any third pitch, for that matter—is still a nearly null set. Gausman continues to survive as he always has, on a competent fastball and a devastating splitter. You might think this sounds like a profile ideal for a high-leverage reliever, perhaps even a closer. In fact, he was the closest thing the Giants had to a rotation anchor, where his two-pitch act enjoyed the spacious coordinates of Oracle Park (and a number of pitcher's parks in the West) enough to make him the de facto ace of a beleaguered staff. Gausman's acceptance of a qualifying offer for 2021 suggests that the current formula solves a problem for both sides.

YEAR	TEAM	LVL	AGE	WHIP	ERA	DRA-	WARP	MPH	FB%	WHF	CSP
2018	BAL	MLB	27	1.38	4.43	98	1.3	96.8	58.8%	24.7%	
2018	ATL	MLB	27	1.14	2.87	69	1.5	96.2	57.0%	24.9%	
2019	GWN	AAA	28	1.00	2.57	53	0.3				
2019	ATL	MLB	28	1.49	6.19	106	0.4	96.6	56.6%	28.3%	
2019	CIN	MLB	28	1.16	4.03	57	0.7	96.6	56.4%	36.9%	
2020	SF	MLB	29	1.11	3.62	73	1.4	97.5	51.1%	33.1%	
2021 FS	SF	MLB	30	1.22	3.39	86	2.6	96.9	55.4%	29.4%	46.8%
2021 DC	SF	MLB	30	1.22	3.39	86	2.5	96.9	55.4%	29.4%	46.8%

Kevin Gausman, continued

Pitch Shape vs LHH

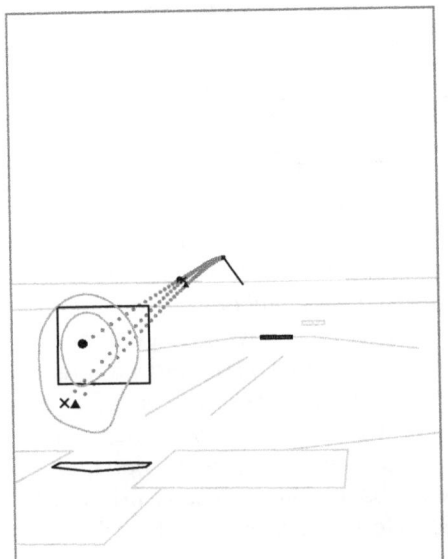

Pitch Shape vs RHH

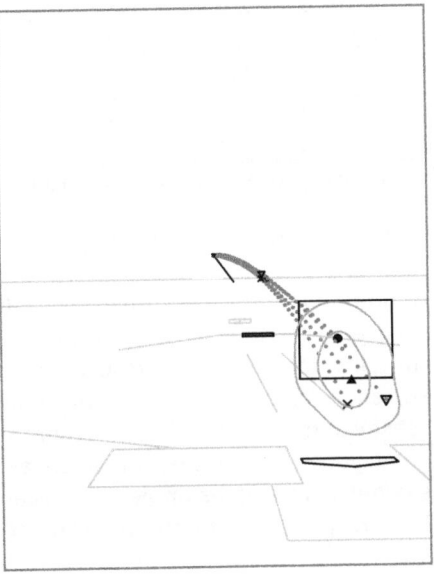

Type	Frequency	Velocity	H Movement	V Movement
● Fastball	51.1%	95.1 [108]	-9.3 [88]	-12.7 [107]
▲ Changeup	12.9%	84.6 [98]	-9.9 [110]	-24.6 [108]
✕ Splitter	29.2%	84 [95]	-11.9 [85]	-32.6 [89]
▽ Slider	6.8%	81.9 [91]	2.3 [89]	-36.3 [93]

Trevor Gott RHP

Born: 08/26/92 Age: 28 Bats: R Throws: R
Height: 5'10" Weight: 182 Origin: Round 6, 2013 Draft (#178 overall)

YEAR	TEAM	LVL	AGE	W	L	SV	G	GS	IP	H	HR	BB/9	K/9	K	GB%	BABIP
2018	SYR	AAA	25	1	1	3	28	0	29^1	23	1	2.5	11.7	38	55.7%	.319
2018	WAS	MLB	25	0	2	0	20	0	19	19	4	4.7	7.1	15	56.1%	.283
2019	SF	MLB	26	7	0	1	50	0	52^2	41	4	2.9	9.7	57	42.8%	.278
2020	SF	MLB	27	1	2	4	15	0	11^2	13	7	6.2	6.2	8	20.0%	.182
2021 FS	SF	MLB	28	2	2	0	57	0	50	46	6	3.8	8.7	48	41.9%	.287
2021 DC	SF	MLB	28	2	2	0	51	0	12.7	12	1	3.8	8.7	12	41.9%	.287

Comparables: Yacksel Ríos, Dovydas Neverauskas, Ian Krol

If some small price could wipe the period of August 14- 17 from Gott's memory, he would gladly pay it. In an inning and a third, stretched across three outings—two on consecutive days at home to the A's, and one two days later in Anaheim—he had himself a properly dystopian stretch, giving up 11 earned runs, including five homers. Outside of that cursed half-week, Gott was great, surrendering only two runs in his remaining innings, and even serving an early-season stint as closer. Perhaps there's an object lesson about what happens when you mainly rely on one pitch, even if it's a perfectly good 96 mph four-seamer. It's a small-sample pity, because the back of his baseball card would look awfully pretty on the 2020 line but for a four-day stretch in which Gott got got.

YEAR	TEAM	LVL	AGE	WHIP	ERA	DRA-	WARP	MPH	FB%	WHF	CSP
2018	SYR	AAA	25	1.06	3.68	67	0.6				
2018	WAS	MLB	25	1.53	5.68	136	-0.3	96.3	74.8%	16.9%	
2019	SF	MLB	26	1.10	4.44	79	0.9	96.1	77.2%	23.6%	
2020	SF	MLB	27	1.80	10.03	231	-0.7	97.2	64.1%	24.7%	
2021 FS	SF	MLB	28	1.35	4.13	99	0.3	96.4	73.8%	23.1%	48.2%
2021 DC	SF	MLB	28	1.35	4.13	99	0.1	96.4	73.8%	23.1%	48.2%

Trevor Gott, continued

Pitch Shape vs LHH	Pitch Shape vs RHH
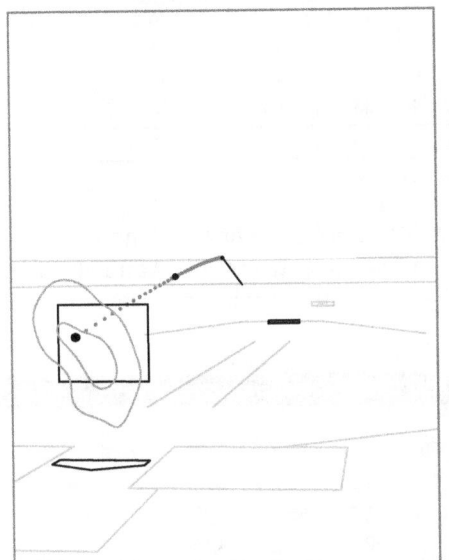	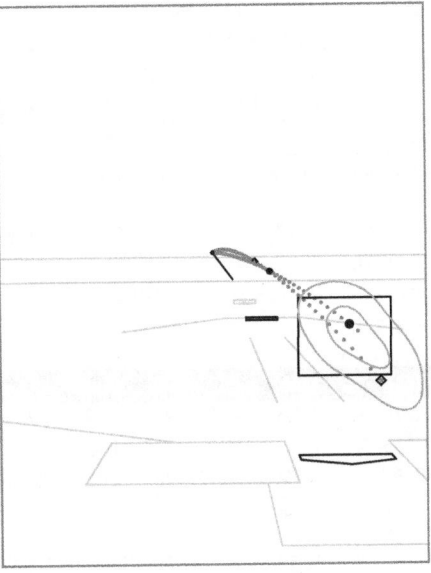

Type	Frequency	Velocity	H Movement	V Movement
● Fastball	63.6%	95.5 [109]	-8.3 [92]	-14 [103]
▽ Slider	7.8%	90.4 [129]	2.1 [88]	-23.7 [129]
◇ Curveball	25.3%	82.4 [115]	10.7 [113]	-45 [108]

Dominic Leone RHP

Born: 10/26/91   Age: 29   Bats: R   Throws: R
Height: 5'10"   Weight: 215   Origin: Round 16, 2012 Draft (#491 overall)

YEAR	TEAM	LVL	AGE	W	L	SV	G	GS	IP	H	HR	BB/9	K/9	K	GB%	BABIP
2018	MEM	AAA	26	1	1	0	10	0	10	14	3	5.4	6.3	7	37.1%	.344
2018	STL	MLB	26	1	2	0	29	0	24	27	3	3.0	9.8	26	30.6%	.353
2019	MEM	AAA	27	1	0	0	23	0	31^2	20	3	4.0	11.9	42	33.3%	.246
2019	STL	MLB	27	1	0	1	40	0	40^2	39	9	4.9	10.2	46	38.4%	.294
2020	CLE	MLB	28	0	0	0	12	0	9^2	14	3	4.7	14.9	16	30.8%	.478
2021 FS	SF	MLB	29	2	2	0	57	0	50	44	8	4.2	10.5	58	36.5%	.293

Comparables: Shawn Armstrong, Cam Bedrosian, Taylor Williams

Leone elevated his slider to primary pitch status for the first time and with good reason: he drew whiffs on two-thirds of swings, struck out 14 and allowed only two singles. The results from his collective fastballs raise the question: can he be a slider-*only* pitcher?

YEAR	TEAM	LVL	AGE	WHIP	ERA	DRA-	WARP	MPH	FB%	WHF	CSP
2018	MEM	AAA	26	2.00	7.20	67	0.2				
2018	STL	MLB	26	1.46	4.50	90	0.2	95.8	95.4%	29.8%	
2019	MEM	AAA	27	1.07	2.84	46	1.2				
2019	STL	MLB	27	1.50	5.53	116	-0.1	95.7	83.7%	30.3%	
2020	CLE	MLB	28	1.97	8.38	93	0.1	96.2	64.4%	36.8%	
2021 FS	SF	MLB	29	1.35	4.04	95	0.4	95.8	80.8%	31.9%	40.4%

Dominic Leone, continued

Pitch Shape vs LHH

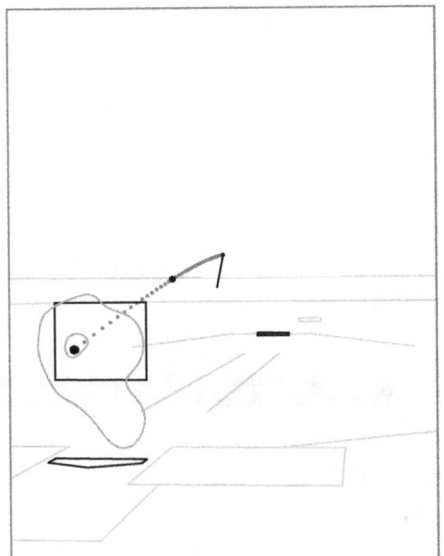

Pitch Shape vs RHH

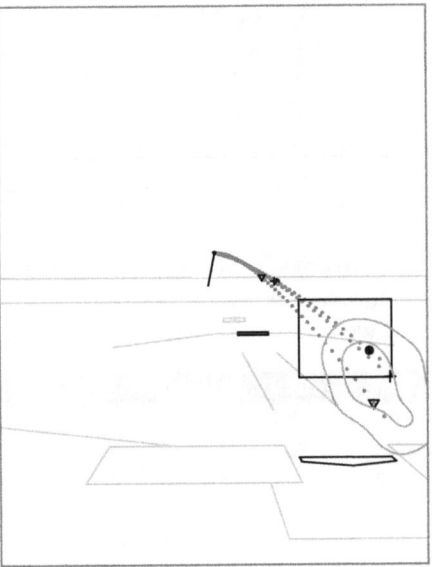

Type	Frequency	Velocity	H Movement	V Movement
● Fastball	33.5%	94.9 [107]	-4.8 [109]	-14.1 [103]
+ Cutter	30.9%	91.1 [117]	2.6 [104]	-23 [105]
▽ Slider	35.6%	84.4 [102]	4.4 [97]	-37.1 [90]

San Francisco Giants 2021

Zack Littell   RHP
Born: 10/05/95   Age: 25   Bats: R   Throws: R
Height: 6'4"   Weight: 220   Origin: Round 11, 2013 Draft (#327 overall)

YEAR	TEAM	LVL	AGE	W	L	SV	G	GS	IP	H	HR	BB/9	K/9	K	GB%	BABIP
2018	CHA	AA	22	0	3	0	5	5	23	28	3	2.7	12.5	32	34.4%	.446
2018	ROC	AAA	22	6	6	0	19	15	106	100	5	3.4	8.3	98	39.5%	.310
2018	MIN	MLB	22	0	2	0	8	2	20^1	25	3	4.9	6.2	14	43.1%	.324
2019	ROC	AAA	23	3	3	1	20	7	63	55	11	3.6	9.7	68	47.9%	.278
2019	MIN	MLB	23	6	0	0	29	0	37	34	4	2.2	7.8	32	38.1%	.300
2020	MIN	MLB	24	0	0	0	6	0	6^1	12	5	4.3	4.3	3	33.3%	.368
2021 FS	SF	MLB	25	2	3	0	57	0	50	49	8	3.4	8.1	45	41.3%	.289

Comparables: Touki Toussaint, Kyle Ryan, Robert Gsellman

We're not sure whether Littell will spend most of his time hopping back and forth between the majors and Triple-A or the majors and an alternate training site; we're considerably more sure that he'll be hopping in either case.

YEAR	TEAM	LVL	AGE	WHIP	ERA	DRA-	WARP	MPH	FB%	WHF	CSP
2018	CHA	AA	22	1.52	5.87	78	0.4				
2018	ROC	AAA	22	1.32	3.57	86	1.4				
2018	MIN	MLB	22	1.77	6.20	149	-0.4	94.6	58.5%	17.9%	
2019	ROC	AAA	23	1.27	3.71	68	2.0				
2019	MIN	MLB	23	1.16	2.68	111	0.0	96.1	49.1%	27.3%	
2020	MIN	MLB	24	2.37	9.95	163	-0.2	95.8	54.7%	13.3%	
2021 FS	SF	MLB	25	1.36	4.58	106	0.1	95.7	52.3%	22.6%	50.8%

Zack Littell, continued

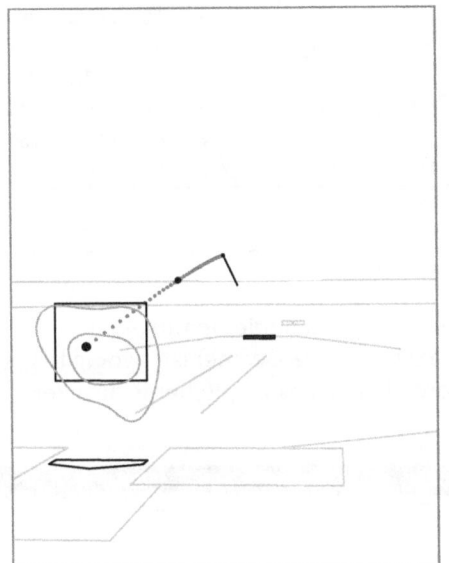

Pitch Shape vs LHH

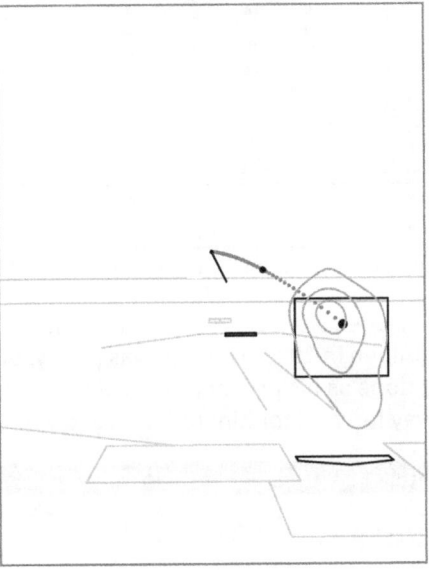

Pitch Shape vs RHH

Type	Frequency	Velocity	H Movement	V Movement
● Fastball	54.7%	94.1 [105]	-6.7 [100]	-12.5 [108]
▽ Slider	42.7%	89 [123]	-0.9 [77]	-24.2 [128]

Conner Menez LHP

Born: 05/29/95 Age: 26 Bats: L Throws: L
Height: 6'2" Weight: 206 Origin: Round 14, 2016 Draft (#425 overall)

YEAR	TEAM	LVL	AGE	W	L	SV	G	GS	IP	H	HR	BB/9	K/9	K	GB%	BABIP
2018	SJ	HI-A	23	2	5	0	11	11	50^1	48	2	3.8	12.5	70	44.1%	.374
2018	RIC	AA	23	6	4	0	15	15	74	73	1	4.1	11.2	92	37.3%	.381
2018	SAC	AAA	23	1	1	0	2	2	11	6	0	4.1	7.4	9	50.0%	.214
2019	RIC	AA	24	3	3	0	11	11	59^2	37	5	3.0	10.6	70	35.7%	.237
2019	SAC	AAA	24	3	1	0	12	11	61^1	60	12	4.4	12.3	84	32.0%	.345
2019	SF	MLB	24	0	1	0	8	3	17	13	4	6.4	11.6	22	28.2%	.265
2020	SF	MLB	25	1	0	0	7	0	11^1	6	2	4.0	6.4	8	29.0%	.143
2021 FS	SF	MLB	26	9	8	0	26	26	150	127	21	4.5	9.7	161	35.0%	.275
2021 DC	SF	MLB	26	3	3	0	21	8	51.7	44	7	4.5	9.7	55	35.0%	.275

Comparables: Matt Hall, Gregory Soto, Anthony Misiewicz

Menez did little to separate himself from the glut of lefties in the Giants bullpen in 2020. The ERA was pretty, but a 92 mph four-seamer isn't going to get it done as his primary pitch. Mixing in more of his breaking pitches is the likely way forward for him to find leg room.

YEAR	TEAM	LVL	AGE	WHIP	ERA	DRA-	WARP	MPH	FB%	WHF	CSP
2018	SJ	HI-A	23	1.37	4.83	67	1.1				
2018	RIC	AA	23	1.45	4.38	84	1.2				
2018	SAC	AAA	23	1.00	3.27	82	0.2				
2019	RIC	AA	24	0.96	2.72	71	1.1				
2019	SAC	AAA	24	1.47	4.84	78	1.7				
2019	SF	MLB	24	1.47	5.29	83	0.3	92.7	61.2%	27.9%	
2020	SF	MLB	25	0.97	2.38	128	-0.1	93.1	54.4%	20.3%	
2021 FS	SF	MLB	26	1.35	4.09	98	1.6	92.9	58.2%	24.5%	46.1%
2021 DC	SF	MLB	26	1.35	4.09	98	0.4	92.9	58.2%	24.5%	46.1%

Conner Menez, continued

Pitch Shape vs LHH

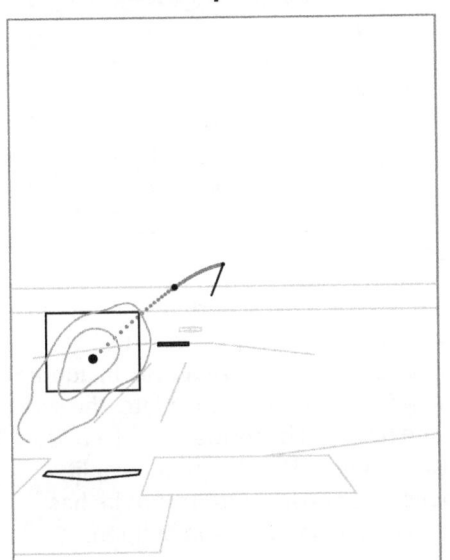

Pitch Shape vs RHH

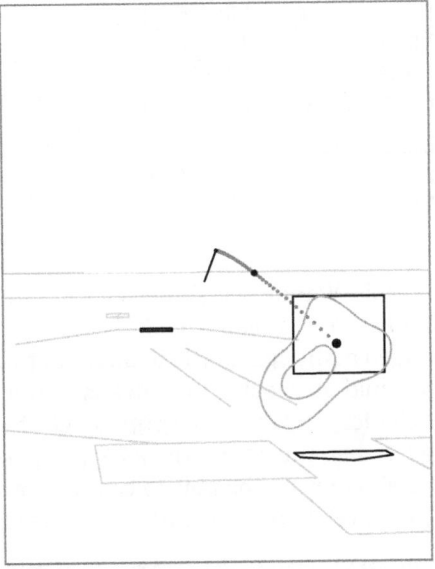

Type	Frequency	Velocity	H Movement	V Movement
● Fastball	54.4%	91.8 [97]	4.7 [110]	-15.1 [100]
▽ Slider	26.0%	84.2 [101]	-5.3 [100]	-33.7 [100]
◇ Curveball	16.6%	80.9 [109]	-7.6 [100]	-42.3 [114]

Wandy Peralta   LHP

Born: 07/27/91   Age: 29   Bats: L   Throws: L
Height: 6'0"   Weight: 217   Origin: International Free Agent, 2009

YEAR	TEAM	LVL	AGE	W	L	SV	G	GS	IP	H	HR	BB/9	K/9	K	GB%	BABIP
2018	LOU	AAA	26	1	0	0	13	0	14^1	13	1	4.4	6.3	10	54.8%	.300
2018	CIN	MLB	26	2	2	0	59	0	45^1	58	2	6.2	6.2	31	47.2%	.350
2019	LOU	AAA	27	0	0	0	12	0	11	11	0	0.8	5.7	7	48.6%	.314
2019	CIN	MLB	27	1	1	0	39	0	34	36	10	4.0	7.1	27	45.8%	.268
2019	SF	MLB	27	0	0	0	8	0	5^2	4	1	1.6	7.9	5	73.3%	.214
2020	SF	MLB	28	1	1	0	25	0	27^1	22	3	3.6	8.2	25	44.7%	.260
2021 FS	SF	MLB	29	2	2	0	57	0	50	48	5	4.5	8.1	45	47.9%	.298
2021 DC	SF	MLB	29	2	2	0	57	0	51.7	50	6	4.5	8.1	46	47.9%	.298

Comparables: Austin Brice, Kevin McCarthy, Mike Mayers

While Wandy was something less than magic, he was something more than a LOOGY for the Giants in 2020—a good thing, since the three-batter rule has forced many specialists to adapt to the more demanding LTOGY role. In addition to a mid-90s heater, Peralta has an out pitch for each side of the plate: the slider to lefties, and the changeup to right-handed hitters. The former is still a better pitch than the latter, which keeps up a visible, if not extreme, platoon split. Peralta may not be able to cast strong spells on opposing hitters, but he has enough skill to conjure at least one more year in a major-league bullpen.

YEAR	TEAM	LVL	AGE	WHIP	ERA	DRA-	WARP	MPH	FB%	WHF	CSP
2018	LOU	AAA	26	1.40	3.14	80	0.2				
2018	CIN	MLB	26	1.96	5.36	168	-1.4	97.2	48.8%	23.0%	
2019	LOU	AAA	27	1.09	3.27	80	0.2				
2019	CIN	MLB	27	1.50	6.09	138	-0.5	96.8	34.6%	32.3%	
2019	SF	MLB	27	0.88	3.18	59	0.2	97.2	48.8%	36.1%	
2020	SF	MLB	28	1.21	3.29	90	0.4	96.0	35.4%	29.0%	
2021 FS	SF	MLB	29	1.48	4.48	104	0.1	96.6	39.0%	28.9%	44.6%
2021 DC	SF	MLB	29	1.48	4.48	104	0.1	96.6	39.0%	28.9%	44.6%

Wandy Peralta, continued

Pitch Shape vs LHH

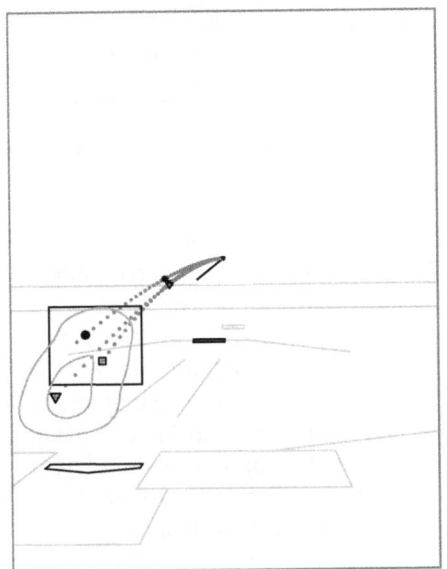

Pitch Shape vs RHH

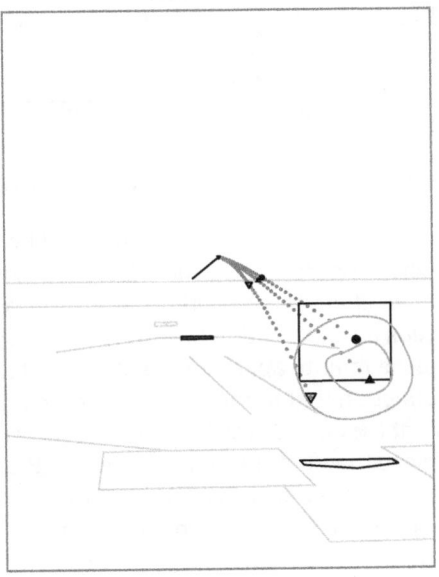

Type	Frequency	Velocity	H Movement	V Movement
● Fastball	23.2%	94.8 [107]	8.8 [90]	-14 [103]
□ Sinker	12.1%	94.6 [111]	13.2 [99]	-18 [108]
▲ Changeup	31.4%	87.6 [110]	15.1 [82]	-26.3 [103]
▽ Slider	33.0%	87.5 [116]	-1.2 [85]	-27.8 [117]

Tyler Rogers RHP

Born: 12/17/90 Age: 30 Bats: R Throws: R
Height: 6'3" Weight: 181 Origin: Round 10, 2013 Draft (#312 overall)

YEAR	TEAM	LVL	AGE	W	L	SV	G	GS	IP	H	HR	BB/9	K/9	K	GB%	BABIP
2018	SAC	AAA	27	3	2	3	51	0	67²	50	4	3.1	8.0	60	60.5%	.257
2019	SAC	AAA	28	4	2	5	49	1	62	59	6	4.1	8.0	55	61.5%	.303
2019	SF	MLB	28	2	0	0	17	0	17²	12	0	1.5	8.2	16	68.0%	.245
2020	SF	MLB	29	3	3	3	29	0	28	31	2	1.9	8.7	27	53.5%	.349
2021 FS	SF	MLB	30	2	2	13	57	0	50	47	4	2.9	8.0	44	57.1%	.296
2021 DC	SF	MLB	30	2	2	13	57	0	58	55	5	2.9	8.0	51	57.1%	.296

Comparables: Eric Yardley, Emilio Pagán, Mike Morin

It's de rigueur for any mention of Rogers to mention his older twin, Taylor, who slings filth from the left side for the Twins. These stories often comment on how different the brothers are, and isn't that just *weird*? Rarely do journalists seek an explanation for this radical disparity. Even though the twins were born just a minute apart, Tyler suffers acutely from *younger twin syndrome*, an affliction that manifests in acts of rebellion that are so mild and so inoffensive that they can scarcely be read as such. This helps explain the little-seen back piece that features a full portrait of Brad Ziegler in mid-submarine delivery, emblazoned with "LIVIN' FREE AT 83" in Old English script. Some rebels are without a cause, but Rogers has made his fight very clear: swim against the current of extreme velocity long enough to carve out a successful role in a big-league bullpen with his funky delivery and excellent control. There's no indication that Rogers is close to burning out; we'll have to see whether or not he fades away.

YEAR	TEAM	LVL	AGE	WHIP	ERA	DRA-	WARP	MPH	FB%	WHF	CSP
2018	SAC	AAA	27	1.08	2.13	76	1.2				
2019	SAC	AAA	28	1.40	4.21	82	1.4				
2019	SF	MLB	28	0.85	1.02	81	0.3	83.8	67.1%	16.5%	
2020	SF	MLB	29	1.32	4.50	79	0.6	84.1	64.2%	24.2%	
2021 FS	SF	MLB	30	1.28	3.59	89	0.5	84.0	65.0%	22.1%	53.3%
2021 DC	SF	MLB	30	1.28	3.59	89	0.6	84.0	65.0%	22.1%	53.3%

Tyler Rogers, continued

Pitch Shape vs LHH

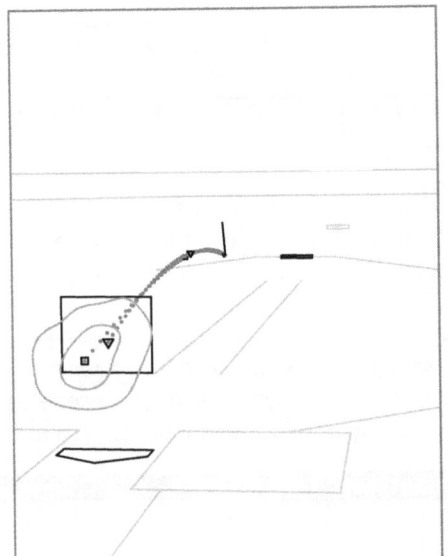

Pitch Shape vs RHH

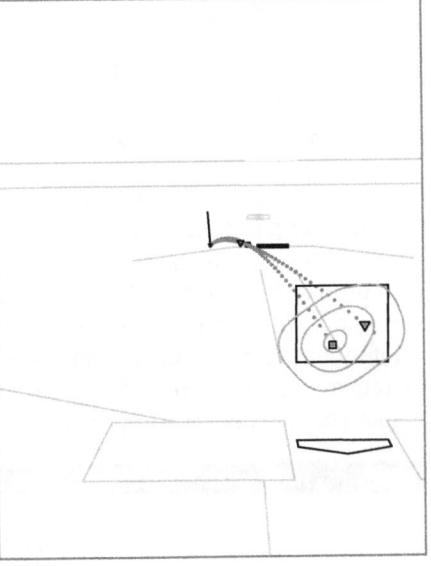

Type	Frequency	Velocity	H Movement	V Movement
☐ Sinker	63.8%	82.4 [49]	-3 [174]	-47 [14]
▽ Slider	35.6%	71.4 [44]	11.6 [124]	-37.8 [88]

Jeff Samardzija   RHP

Born: 01/23/85   Age: 36   Bats: R   Throws: R
Height: 6'4"   Weight: 233   Origin: Round 5, 2006 Draft (#149 overall)

YEAR	TEAM	LVL	AGE	W	L	SV	G	GS	IP	H	HR	BB/9	K/9	K	GB%	BABIP
2018	SAC	AAA	33	0	2	0	4	4	17	17	5	1.6	10.6	20	40.4%	.286
2018	SF	MLB	33	1	5	0	10	10	44²	47	6	5.2	6.0	30	28.9%	.289
2019	SF	MLB	34	11	12	0	32	32	181¹	152	28	2.4	6.9	140	36.1%	.242
2020	SF	MLB	35	0	2	0	4	4	16²	21	7	2.2	3.2	6	20.0%	.241
2021 FS	SF	MLB	36	8	9	0	26	26	150	159	28	2.7	6.4	106	33.7%	.282

Comparables: Ian Kennedy, Mike Fiers, Aníbal Sánchez

For several years, Shark has been more tail than teeth—as the fastball has lost bite, the long, last phase of his career has suffered from injury setbacks, home-run troubles and sinker-smashing hitters, all of these woes intermittently obscured by his ability to log innings while swimming just above the ERA waterline. When sharks are near the end, do they disappear into the depths or hunt for easier prey closer to shore? Released by the Giants into free-agent waters at the end of the season, Samardzija will no longer be the apex predator; instead he'll be fighting for his food in a crowded and inhospitable ecosystem.

YEAR	TEAM	LVL	AGE	WHIP	ERA	DRA-	WARP	MPH	FB%	WHF	CSP
2018	SAC	AAA	33	1.18	5.29	86	0.3				
2018	SF	MLB	33	1.63	6.25	160	-1.0	95.1	63.2%	20.8%	
2019	SF	MLB	34	1.11	3.52	90	2.7	93.8	69.0%	20.0%	
2020	SF	MLB	35	1.50	9.72	219	-0.9	92.5	54.0%	13.4%	
2021 FS	SF	MLB	36	1.36	4.74	114	0.3	93.8	66.6%	19.3%	48.0%

Jeff Samardzija, continued

Pitch Shape vs LHH	Pitch Shape vs RHH
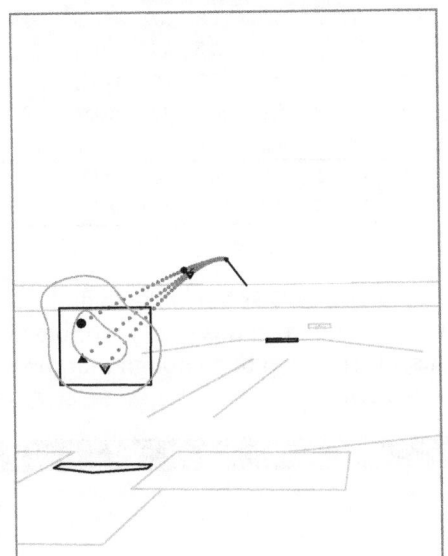	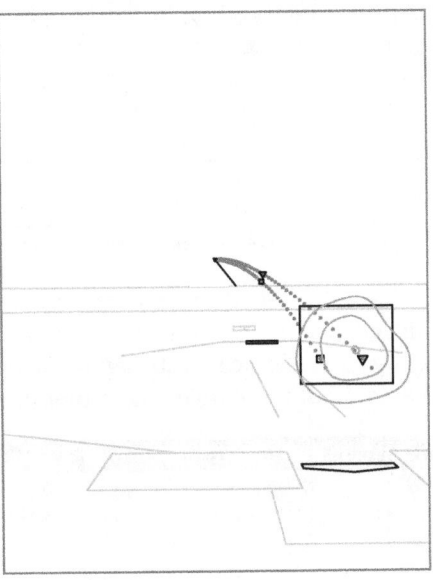

Type	Frequency	Velocity	H Movement	V Movement
● Fastball	18.1%	90.2 [92]	-9.8 [85]	-16 [98]
☐ Sinker	18.5%	91 [92]	-15 [86]	-20.1 [101]
+ Cutter	17.4%	87.3 [94]	-2.3 [73]	-19.8 [117]
▲ Changeup	14.1%	82.6 [90]	-13.7 [90]	-28.1 [98]
✕ Splitter	6.0%	81.8 [84]	-7.6 [101]	-30.8 [95]
▽ Slider	25.8%	84.2 [101]	-1.3 [75]	-27.3 [119]

Sam Selman LHP

Born: 11/14/90 Age: 30 Bats: R Throws: L
Height: 6'2" Weight: 198 Origin: Round 2, 2012 Draft (#66 overall)

YEAR	TEAM	LVL	AGE	W	L	SV	G	GS	IP	H	HR	BB/9	K/9	K	GB%	BABIP
2018	NWA	AA	27	1	2	0	12	0	12^1	12	0	8.0	15.3	21	33.3%	.444
2018	OMA	AAA	27	0	2	0	23	0	28^1	22	0	6.0	11.8	37	43.3%	.328
2019	RIC	AA	28	0	0	0	4	0	7	3	0	1.3	16.7	13	50.0%	.273
2019	SAC	AAA	28	3	2	0	39	1	48	25	4	3.0	15.2	81	41.4%	.253
2019	SF	MLB	28	0	0	0	10	0	10^1	6	2	5.2	8.7	10	30.8%	.174
2020	SF	MLB	29	1	1	1	24	0	19^1	13	2	4.2	10.7	23	31.2%	.244
2021 FS	*SF*	*MLB*	*30*	*2*	*2*	*0*	*57*	*0*	*50*	*40*	*6*	*4.8*	*11.9*	*66*	*38.5%*	*.294*
2021 DC	*SF*	*MLB*	*30*	*2*	*2*	*0*	*51*	*0*	*51.7*	*42*	*6*	*4.8*	*11.9*	*68*	*38.5%*	*.294*

Comparables: Hoby Milner, Eric Yardley, Dakota Bacus

Like scores of other pitchers, Selman should be a LOOGY but woke to find himself in a three-batter-minimum world. Even though he was pretty hittable by righty bats, and he still struggles with walks, his slider is good enough that the Giants should probably hold rather than sell, man.

YEAR	TEAM	LVL	AGE	WHIP	ERA	DRA-	WARP	MPH	FB%	WHF	CSP
2018	NWA	AA	27	1.86	6.57	84	0.1				
2018	OMA	AAA	27	1.45	4.13	62	0.7				
2019	RIC	AA	28	0.57	0.00	45	0.2				
2019	SAC	AAA	28	0.85	2.06	14	2.6				
2019	SF	MLB	28	1.16	4.35	111	0.0	92.0	42.5%	31.1%	
2020	SF	MLB	29	1.14	3.72	92	0.3	92.8	41.0%	29.9%	
2021 FS	*SF*	*MLB*	*30*	*1.34*	*3.88*	*92*	*0.5*	*92.6*	*41.4%*	*30.2%*	*46.5%*
2021 DC	*SF*	*MLB*	*30*	*1.34*	*3.88*	*92*	*0.5*	*92.6*	*41.4%*	*30.2%*	*46.5%*

Sam Selman, continued

Pitch Shape vs LHH

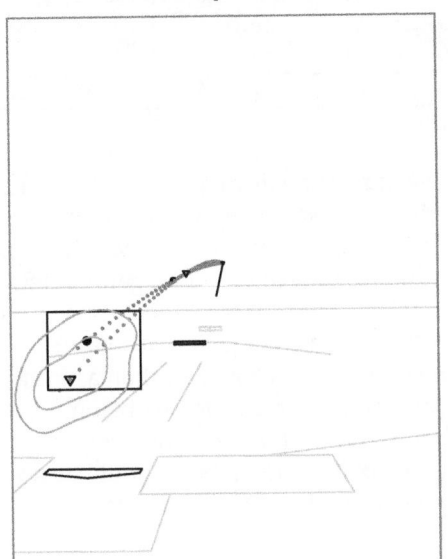

Pitch Shape vs RHH

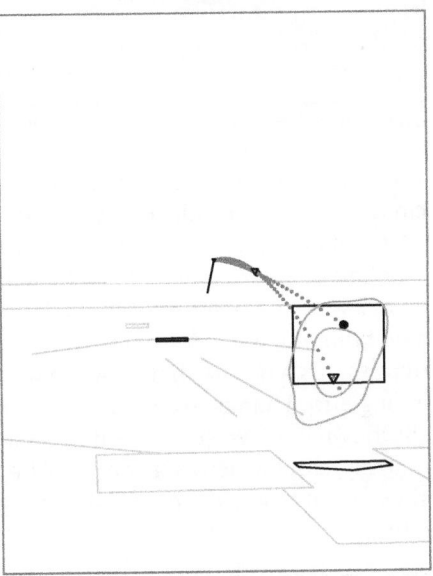

Type	Frequency	Velocity	H Movement	V Movement
● Fastball	41.0%	91.2 [95]	2.6 [120]	-15.3 [100]
▽ Slider	59.0%	79.9 [82]	-11.4 [123]	-36.9 [91]

Tony Watson LHP

Born: 05/30/85 Age: 36 Bats: L Throws: L
Height: 6'3" Weight: 224 Origin: Round 9, 2007 Draft (#278 overall)

YEAR	TEAM	LVL	AGE	W	L	SV	G	GS	IP	H	HR	BB/9	K/9	K	GB%	BABIP
2018	SF	MLB	33	4	6	0	72	0	66	54	4	1.9	9.8	72	43.7%	.299
2019	SF	MLB	34	2	2	0	60	0	54	56	9	2.0	6.8	41	45.1%	.290
2020	SF	MLB	35	1	0	2	21	0	18	13	3	1.5	7.5	15	50.0%	.196
2021 FS	SF	MLB	36	2	2	0	57	0	50	48	6	2.2	7.5	41	45.9%	.290

Comparables: Brandon Kintzler, Pedro Strop, Joe Smith

It's easy for statheads to scoff at the save: it's a statistic more dependent on circumstance than skill. Everyone knows this. But Watson may have entered 2020 thinking, after two partial seasons as a closer in Pittsburgh a few years ago, that he may never again get that catcher's handshake after a close game. A lefty who, like so many others, has backgrounded the sinker, Watson now survives on a diet that mixes his former bread-and-butter with a changeup that stymies righties. It's a profile that makes him more than a LOOGY but less than a ninth-inning arm. Thanks to a combination of fluid bullpen roles and no obvious shutdown guy, Watson logged not one, but two saves for the Giants. While these unlikely, stochastic saves may well be the last of his career, there should be no shortage of teams needing a skilled, seasoned lefty for innings other than the ninth.

YEAR	TEAM	LVL	AGE	WHIP	ERA	DRA-	WARP	MPH	FB%	WHF	CSP
2018	SF	MLB	33	1.03	2.59	74	1.2	94.2	51.1%	27.0%	
2019	SF	MLB	34	1.26	4.17	114	-0.1	94.5	51.5%	25.9%	
2020	SF	MLB	35	0.89	2.50	99	0.2	91.4	37.9%	27.2%	
2021 FS	SF	MLB	36	1.21	3.57	87	0.6	93.6	48.0%	26.5%	49.4%

Tony Watson, continued

Pitch Shape vs LHH

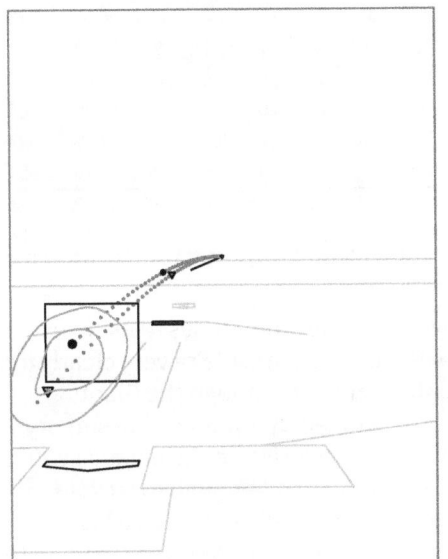

Pitch Shape vs RHH

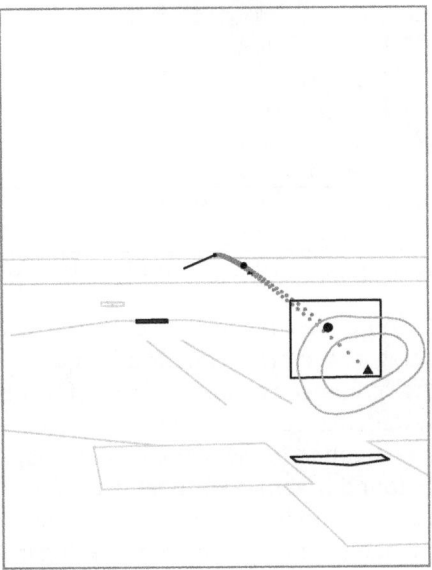

Type	Frequency	Velocity	H Movement	V Movement
● Fastball	30.0%	89.7 [91]	13 [70]	-21.4 [82]
□ Sinker	7.9%	90 [88]	16.4 [75]	-24.8 [86]
▲ Changeup	48.2%	84 [96]	17 [72]	-28.3 [98]
▽ Slider	13.9%	81.1 [87]	-2.6 [90]	-35.4 [95]

San Francisco Giants 2021

Logan Webb RHP
Born: 11/18/96 Age: 24 Bats: R Throws: R
Height: 6'1" Weight: 220 Origin: Round 4, 2014 Draft (#118 overall)

YEAR	TEAM	LVL	AGE	W	L	SV	G	GS	IP	H	HR	BB/9	K/9	K	GB%	BABIP
2018	SJ	HI-A	21	1	3	0	21	20	74	54	2	4.4	9.0	74	46.9%	.275
2018	RIC	AA	21	1	2	0	6	6	30²	30	4	3.2	7.6	26	50.0%	.292
2019	AUG	LO-A	22	1	0	0	2	1	10	4	0	2.7	8.1	9	58.3%	.167
2019	RIC	AA	22	1	4	0	8	7	41¹	41	2	2.6	10.2	47	65.0%	.331
2019	SAC	AAA	22	0	0	0	1	1	7	7	0	0.0	9.0	7	63.2%	.368
2019	SF	MLB	22	2	3	0	8	8	39²	44	5	3.2	8.4	37	47.5%	.333
2020	SF	MLB	23	3	4	0	13	11	54¹	61	4	4.0	7.6	46	52.1%	.350
2021 FS	SF	MLB	24	9	8	0	26	26	150	145	18	4.0	8.2	135	51.1%	.294
2021 DC	SF	MLB	24	7	7	0	25	24	114	110	14	4.0	8.2	103	51.1%	.294

Comparables: Scott Olsen, Patrick Corbin, Joe Ross

Sometimes the narrative doesn't always go to plan; sometimes it just ends up being a little more circuitous, requiring patience and faith. We're very clearly in the "patience and faith" phase of Webb's story. His trip through the Giants system has been far from a fairy tale: He was derailed by Tommy John surgery, then nabbed for an 80-game PED suspension. Upon arrival in the majors in 2019, he found that mid-90s heat with spotty command wasn't enough to sustain success, and in 2020 he dialed down the four-seamer usage to feature his changeup more prominently. Going into his age-24 season, Webb may not quite be ready for a full-time rotation gig, but he should still have plenty of chances to bend his narrative arc toward happier outcomes.

YEAR	TEAM	LVL	AGE	WHIP	ERA	DRA-	WARP	MPH	FB%	WHF	CSP
2018	SJ	HI-A	21	1.22	1.82	123	-0.7				
2018	RIC	AA	21	1.34	3.82	80	0.6				
2019	AUG	LO-A	22	0.70	0.90	62	0.2				
2019	RIC	AA	22	1.28	2.18	89	0.3				
2019	SAC	AAA	22	1.00	1.29	64	0.2				
2019	SF	MLB	22	1.46	5.22	85	0.7	94.6	56.4%	22.8%	
2020	SF	MLB	23	1.56	5.47	97	0.6	94.8	48.6%	22.9%	
2021 FS	SF	MLB	24	1.42	4.30	102	1.3	94.7	51.0%	22.9%	46.6%
2021 DC	SF	MLB	24	1.42	4.30	102	1.0	94.7	51.0%	22.9%	46.6%

Logan Webb, continued

Pitch Shape vs LHH

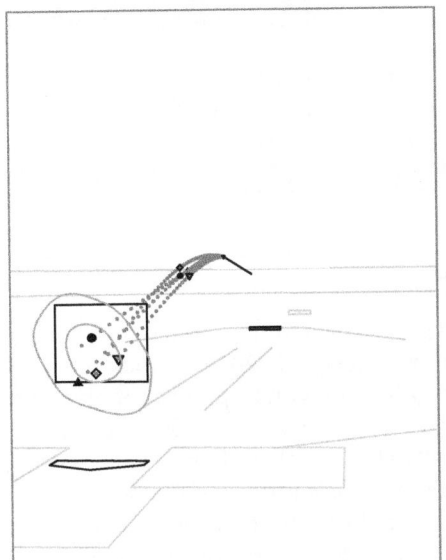

Pitch Shape vs RHH

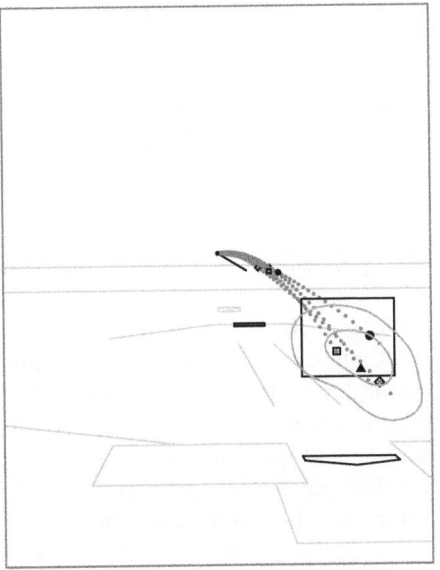

Type	Frequency	Velocity	H Movement	V Movement
● Fastball	31.9%	93.2 [102]	-7.7 [95]	-16.8 [95]
□ Sinker	16.5%	91.8 [97]	-15.3 [84]	-24.4 [87]
▲ Changeup	30.6%	84.7 [98]	-11.2 [103]	-35.7 [77]
▽ Slider	5.3%	90.5 [129]	-1.3 [75]	-22.4 [133]
◇ Curveball	15.3%	81.5 [111]	11 [114]	-38.1 [123]

Matt Wisler RHP

Born: 09/12/92   Age: 28   Bats: R   Throws: R
Height: 6'3"   Weight: 215   Origin: Round 7, 2011 Draft (#233 overall)

YEAR	TEAM	LVL	AGE	W	L	SV	G	GS	IP	H	HR	BB/9	K/9	K	GB%	BABIP
2018	GWN	AAA	25	4	4	0	13	13	70	79	6	1.8	8.4	65	45.8%	.354
2018	LOU	AAA	25	1	1	0	8	2	19^2	19	0	1.4	9.6	21	35.7%	.339
2018	ATL	MLB	25	1	1	0	7	3	26^2	30	6	1.7	7.1	21	27.9%	.300
2018	CIN	MLB	25	0	0	0	11	0	13^1	11	2	1.4	7.4	11	39.0%	.237
2019	SD	MLB	26	2	2	0	21	0	29	34	5	3.1	10.6	34	43.5%	.367
2019	SEA	MLB	26	1	2	0	23	8	22^1	22	5	2.4	11.7	29	26.7%	.309
2020	MIN	MLB	27	0	1	1	18	4	25^1	15	2	5.0	12.4	35	23.2%	.241
2021 FS	*SF*	*MLB*	*28*	*2*	*2*	*3*	*57*	*0*	*50*	*45*	*8*	*3.1*	*10.0*	*55*	*33.8%*	*.288*
2021 DC	*SF*	*MLB*	*28*	*2*	*2*	*3*	*57*	*0*	*58*	*52*	*9*	*3.1*	*10.0*	*64*	*33.8%*	*.288*

Comparables: Robert Stephenson, Archie Bradley, Brett Cecil

    Wisler is your friend who breaks board games by finding a dominant strategy and then steadfastly refusing to do anything different. In 2020, he took pitch spamming to its logical conclusion by firing his slider on 84 percent of his tosses. To put that in context, nobody else throws one even two-thirds of the time, and only Jake McGee throws any pitch (fastball in this case) as often as Wisler uses the slide piece. The plan worked, as the right-hander produced the best numbers of his career and emerged as a valuable multi-inning weapon in a very strong bullpen. Still, it's worth emphasizing just how weird Wisler's transition from generic four-pitch righty to one-trick pony has been. He's very predictable, doesn't have an unusual spin profile, gives up a ton of fly balls and needs to generate a bunch of called strikes and weak contact to make everything work. We're going to need to see this twice before buying in completely but at the very least, Wisler is far more interesting now than he was this time last year. Sometimes the fifth time (or team) is the charm.

YEAR	TEAM	LVL	AGE	WHIP	ERA	DRA-	WARP	MPH	FB%	WHF	CSP
2018	GWN	AAA	25	1.33	4.37	66	1.8				
2018	LOU	AAA	25	1.12	1.83	74	0.4				
2018	ATL	MLB	25	1.31	5.40	89	0.3	94.4	53.4%	22.2%	
2018	CIN	MLB	25	0.97	2.02	95	0.1	93.5	42.1%	23.2%	
2019	SD	MLB	26	1.52	5.28	79	0.5	94.5	28.6%	32.3%	
2019	SEA	MLB	26	1.25	6.04	92	0.2	94.1	29.8%	31.7%	
2020	MIN	MLB	27	1.14	1.07	98	0.2	93.5	16.6%	36.1%	
2021 FS	*SF*	*MLB*	*28*	*1.25*	*3.81*	*95*	*0.4*	*94.1*	*27.9%*	*32.0%*	*47.8%*
2021 DC	*SF*	*MLB*	*28*	*1.25*	*3.81*	*95*	*0.5*	*94.1*	*27.9%*	*32.0%*	*47.8%*

Matt Wisler, continued

Pitch Shape vs LHH

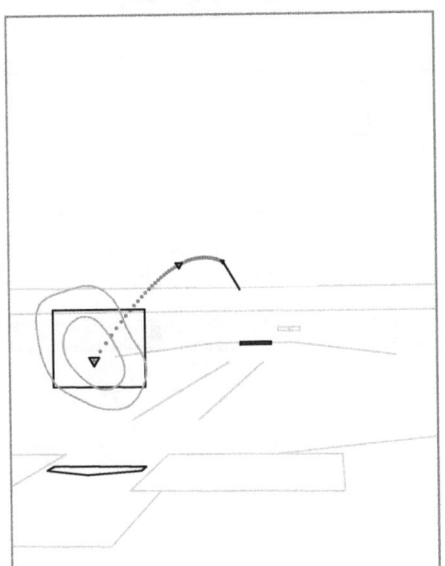

Pitch Shape vs RHH

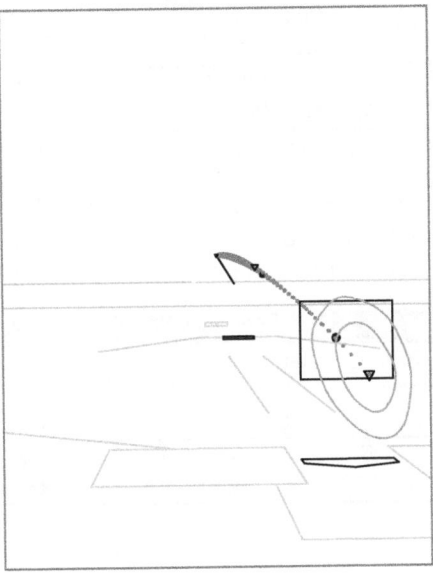

Type	Frequency	Velocity	H Movement	V Movement
● Fastball	16.3%	92.1 [99]	-7.8 [95]	-14.1 [103]
▽ Slider	83.4%	81.5 [89]	9.9 [118]	-38.2 [87]

Alex Wood LHP

Born: 01/12/91 Age: 30 Bats: R Throws: L
Height: 6'4" Weight: 215 Origin: Round 2, 2012 Draft (#85 overall)

YEAR	TEAM	LVL	AGE	W	L	SV	G	GS	IP	H	HR	BB/9	K/9	K	GB%	BABIP
2018	LAD	MLB	27	9	7	0	33	27	151^2	143	14	2.4	8.0	135	48.5%	.295
2019	CIN	MLB	28	1	3	0	7	7	35^2	41	11	2.3	7.6	30	36.3%	.300
2020	LAD	MLB	29	0	1	0	9	2	12^2	17	2	4.3	10.7	15	39.0%	.385
2021 FS	SF	MLB	30	2	2	0	57	0	50	47	6	2.5	8.6	47	44.0%	.293
2021 DC	SF	MLB	30	9	7	0	36	22	126.3	120	16	2.5	8.6	120	44.0%	.293

Comparables: Kevin Gausman, Mike Clevinger, Rafael Montero

His exquisite combination of herk and jerk has afforded Wood a relatively long career, but thanks to his fading stuff and the cinch the league has tightened around situational relievers, he's running out of ways to be valuable.

YEAR	TEAM	LVL	AGE	WHIP	ERA	DRA-	WARP	MPH	FB%	WHF	CSP
2018	LAD	MLB	27	1.21	3.68	76	3.3	91.5	43.0%	23.8%	
2019	CIN	MLB	28	1.40	5.80	129	-0.2	91.1	50.3%	24.9%	
2020	LAD	MLB	29	1.82	6.39	99	0.1	92.3	48.2%	28.7%	
2021 FS	SF	MLB	30	1.23	3.58	90	0.5	91.6	45.9%	25.0%	46.4%
2021 DC	SF	MLB	30	1.23	3.58	90	1.8	91.6	45.9%	25.0%	46.4%

Alex Wood, continued

Pitch Shape vs LHH

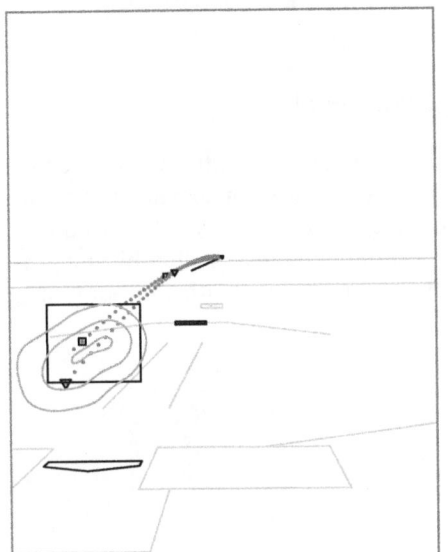

Pitch Shape vs RHH

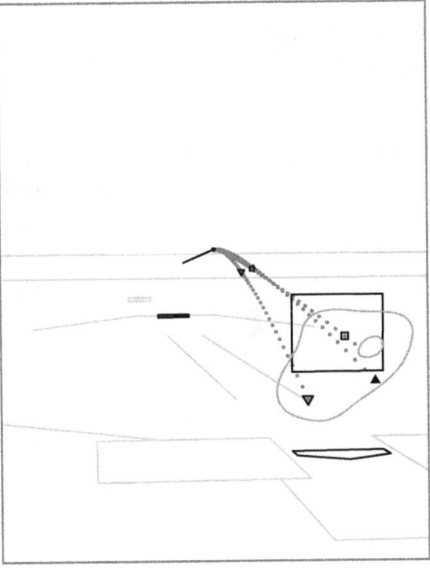

Type	Frequency	Velocity	H Movement	V Movement
☐ Sinker	47.6%	91.1 [93]	11.8 [110]	-17.4 [110]
▲ Changeup	22.7%	84.7 [98]	12.6 [95]	-31.9 [88]
▽ Slider	28.3%	84.6 [103]	0.6 [78]	-34.1 [99]

PLAYER COMMENTS WITHOUT GRAPHS

Patrick Bailey   C
Born: 05/29/99   Age: 22   Bats: S   Throws: R
Height: 6'2"   Weight: 207   Origin: Round 1, 2020 Draft (#13 overall)

Spending a first-round pick on Bailey, a bat-first catcher who is only two years behind a franchise building block at the position, may seem like an inefficiency, until you think for a minute about all the things that can go wrong with catching prospects. Besides, even if Bart pans out as hoped, Bailey's switch-hitting power bat should play somewhere, be it at a different position or with another team.

Brandon Belt 1B

Born: 04/20/88   Age: 33   Bats: L   Throws: L
Height: 6'3"   Weight: 231   Origin: Round 5, 2009 Draft (#147 overall)

YEAR	TEAM	LVL	AGE	PA	R	2B	3B	HR	RBI	BB	K	SB	CS	AVG/OBP/SLG
2018	SF	MLB	30	456	50	18	2	14	46	49	107	4	0	.253/.342/.414
2019	SF	MLB	31	616	76	32	3	17	57	83	127	4	3	.234/.339/.403
2020	SF	MLB	32	179	25	13	1	9	30	30	36	0	0	.309/.425/.591
2021 FS	SF	MLB	33	600	78	25	4	18	74	86	146	3	3	.238/.352/.417
2021 DC	SF	MLB	33	581	75	25	3	18	72	83	141	3	3	.238/.352/.417

Comparables: Derrek Lee, Brian Daubach, Jeff Conine

There was considerable speculation about whether or not the short season would be a net benefit or detriment to the health of pitchers. Would the short stretch help preserve arms that had been habitually overworked? Or would the inconsistent off-season and quick ramp-up lead to more injuries? What we *should* have focused on was whether or not the 60-game season could fall outside of the inevitable, bad-luck injury to Belt, or whether his curse was so strong that he could play a six-game season and still take an unfortunate ball to an unfortunate place, or twist, tear or break something while performing a harmless everyday action. Well, the results are in, and: the 60-game Belt was the best Belt, with him setting career-bests in nearly every rate-based category. It probably didn't hurt that fences were moved to limit the massive right- and center-field acreage in Oracle Park, and (perhaps more significantly) that the closure of the right field archway portholes cut down on winds blowing in from the bay. Nonetheless, Belt was magnificent, and more importantly, injury-free...albeit not by much, as he had surgery to remove a bone spur from his heel two weeks after the conclusion of the season. Perhaps even one additional playoff game would have been a bridge too far. We won't even speculate on adding another hundred games to that total for future seasons, but he'll always have those two beautiful months in 2020.

YEAR	TEAM	LVL	AGE	PA	DRC+	BABIP	BRR	FRAA	WARP
2018	SF	MLB	30	456	107	.311	-0.6	1B(104): 9.9, LF(8): 0.3	2.1
2019	SF	MLB	31	616	105	.275	-2.2	1B(144): 7.2, LF(14): -0.5, RF(1): -0.0	1.9
2020	SF	MLB	32	179	146	.356	-0.8	1B(47): 0.4	1.4
2021 FS	SF	MLB	33	600	115	.295	-0.1	1B 3, LF 0	2.4
2021 DC	SF	MLB	33	581	115	.295	-0.1	1B 3	2.3

San Francisco Giants 2021

Hunter Bishop OF
Born: 06/25/98   Age: 23   Bats: L   Throws: R
Height: 6'5"   Weight: 210   Origin: Round 1, 2019 Draft (#10 overall)

YEAR	TEAM	LVL	AGE	PA	R	2B	3B	HR	RBI	BB	K	SB	CS	AVG/OBP/SLG
2019	GIO	ROK	21	29	4	3	0	1	3	9	11	2	0	.250/.483/.550
2019	SK	SS	21	117	21	1	1	4	9	29	28	4	2	.224/.427/.400
2021 FS	SF	MLB	23	600	52	20	3	11	53	59	217	8	4	.188/.274/.305

Comparables: Rico Noel, Matt Angle, Garrett Hampson

Looking at Bishop's game is like binge-watching *Diners, Drive-Ins, and Dives*. It all looks so tempting, even in its aggressive lack of subtlety. Power from the left side: OFF THE HOOK. Upper-cut swing: MMM-HMMM. Speed: RIGHTEOUS. Lanky, athletic frame: SHUT THE FRONT DOOR. Ability to take a walk: FUNKALICIOUS. Your mouth is already watering, even if your gut tells you that the strikeouts might cause some sharp pains and center field will likely disappear from the menu. Still, for an organization whose outfield is a bit bland yet, Bishop is one prospect who could take the Giants on the express bus to Flavortown.

YEAR	TEAM	LVL	AGE	PA	DRC+	BABIP	BRR	FRAA	WARP
2019	GIO	ROK	21	29		.500			
2019	SK	SS	21	117	176	.278	-0.3	CF(22): -2.2	0.7
2021 FS	SF	MLB	23	600	63	.290	0.6	CF -4	-1.3

Alexander Canario CF
Born: 05/07/00   Age: 21   Bats: R   Throws: R
Height: 6'1"   Weight: 165   Origin: International Free Agent, 2016

YEAR	TEAM	LVL	AGE	PA	R	2B	3B	HR	RBI	BB	K	SB	CS	AVG/OBP/SLG
2018	GIB	ROK	18	208	36	5	2	6	19	27	51	8	5	.250/.357/.403
2019	GIO	ROK	19	46	13	3	1	7	14	2	9	1	0	.395/.435/1.000
2019	SK	SS	19	219	38	17	1	9	40	18	71	3	1	.301/.365/.539
2021 FS	SF	MLB	21	600	45	21	3	9	50	37	211	11	6	.193/.249/.295

Comparables: Greg Halman, Victor Robles, Austin Meadows

A dislocated shoulder during fall instructs, and a subsequent labrum surgery, has pressed the pause button on Canario's development. Power has been the 20-year-old's calling card, so one can only wish him a full recovery before speculating about his future role with the club.

YEAR	TEAM	LVL	AGE	PA	DRC+	BABIP	BRR	FRAA	WARP
2018	GIB	ROK	18	208		.317			
2019	GIO	ROK	19	46		.370			
2019	SK	SS	19	219	158	.419	-1.0	CF(26): -8.1, RF(16): -1.1	0.5
2021 FS	SF	MLB	21	600	48	.292	1.2	CF 0, RF 1	-1.9

Zack Cozart 3B

Born: 08/12/85 Age: 35 Bats: R Throws: R
Height: 6'0" Weight: 205 Origin: Round 2, 2007 Draft (#79 overall)

YEAR	TEAM	LVL	AGE	PA	R	2B	3B	HR	RBI	BB	K	SB	CS	AVG/OBP/SLG
2018	LAA	MLB	32	253	29	13	2	5	18	19	42	0	0	.219/.296/.362
2019	LAA	MLB	33	107	4	2	0	0	7	5	16	0	0	.124/.178/.144
2021 FS	SF	MLB	35	600	59	23	3	15	63	51	118	3	1	.226/.302/.368

Comparables: Clint Barmes, Royce Clayton, Shane Halter

Behold baseball's New Economics: in December of 2019, the Giants traded for Cozart and first-rounder Will Wilson in exchange for extremely minor minor-leaguer Garrett Williams. The Angels were able to clear Cozart's contract in their efforts to free up money for a possible Gerrit Cole signing (which: womp womp). The Giants were happy to take on Cozart's contract, along with his injured shoulder, to acquire Wilson and immediately add a top-five prospect to the system. The pretense of a Cozart comeback was given up in January, when the shortstop-turned-third-baseman was released almost one month to the day after his trade to San Francisco. Farhan Zaidi's effective purchase of a prospect for the cost of a big contract may have laid a blueprint that other clubs will follow. Will this gambit work on anyone but the Angels? We'll find out soon enough.

YEAR	TEAM	LVL	AGE	PA	DRC+	BABIP	BRR	FRAA	WARP
2018	LAA	MLB	32	253	90	.244	-0.2	3B(35): -0.7, 2B(16): -0.2, SS(15): 0.3	0.5
2019	LAA	MLB	33	107	66	.143	0.4	3B(31): 0.5, SS(5): -1.0, 2B(1): -0.1	-0.1
2021 FS	SF	MLB	35	600	87	.262	-0.2	3B 0, SS -2	0.0

Jaylin Davis RF
Born: 07/01/94 Age: 27 Bats: R Throws: R
Height: 5'11" Weight: 205 Origin: Round 24, 2015 Draft (#710 overall)

YEAR	TEAM	LVL	AGE	PA	R	2B	3B	HR	RBI	BB	K	SB	CS	AVG/OBP/SLG
2018	FTM	HI-A	23	227	23	10	0	5	19	23	57	3	2	.271/.354/.397
2018	CHA	AA	23	267	30	14	2	6	34	21	69	5	2	.275/.341/.425
2019	PNS	AA	24	251	34	9	0	10	25	36	64	7	3	.274/.382/.458
2019	ROC	AAA	24	173	39	11	1	15	42	15	46	2	0	.331/.405/.708
2019	SAC	AAA	24	117	21	6	0	10	27	14	28	1	1	.333/.419/.686
2019	SF	MLB	24	47	2	0	0	1	3	3	11	1	2	.167/.255/.238
2020	SF	MLB	25	12	2	0	0	1	1	0	6	0	0	.167/.167/.417
2021 FS	SF	MLB	26	600	76	23	2	25	76	48	219	2	2	.229/.299/.427
2021 DC	SF	MLB	26	31	3	1	0	1	3	2	11	0	0	.229/.299/.427

Comparables: Jason Perry, Adolis Garcia, Michael Reed

The ridiculous excess of 2019 Triple-A batting lines has generated enough disinformation that it's surprising Rachel Maddow hasn't led a week of nightly shows with this issue. We may be sorting through the inflated averages and Ruthian power numbers for a while still, trying to separate good intel from fake news. Davis' case may be one of the easier ones to crack, however: a 2019 that saw him bang 35 homers and maintain a nearly .400 on-base percentage might have been the stuff of momentary headlines, but his limited run in the majors has suggested his story is just another dead-end. With some encouraging indications that Davis has adjusted his swing plane, it may be a little early to consign him to yesterday's news; he will need to show that he can make more regular contact, though, if his major-league career is ever going to make it above the fold.

YEAR	TEAM	LVL	AGE	PA	DRC+	BABIP	BRR	FRAA	WARP
2018	FTM	HI-A	23	227	123	.355	4.1	RF(50): -6.2, LF(2): -0.2	0.3
2018	CHA	AA	23	267	110	.359	-0.2	RF(50): 2.5, CF(1): -0.1	0.5
2019	PNS	AA	24	251	155	.345	-0.2	RF(42): -2.0, LF(8): 0.8, CF(4): 0.4	1.8
2019	ROC	AAA	24	173	159	.387	0.3	RF(32): 2.8, CF(6): 0.5	1.8
2019	SAC	AAA	24	117	138	.375	0.9	RF(16): 3.1, CF(7): 0.6, LF(4): -0.0	1.2
2019	SF	MLB	24	47	68	.200	-0.7	RF(15): -0.5	-0.2
2020	SF	MLB	25	12	81	.200	-0.1	RF(4): -0.0	0.0
2021 FS	SF	MLB	26	600	100	.326	-0.3	RF 7, LF 0	2.0
2021 DC	SF	MLB	26	31	100	.326	0.0	RF 0	0.1

Alex Dickerson LF

Born: 05/26/90   Age: 31   Bats: L   Throws: L
Height: 6'2"   Weight: 226   Origin: Round 3, 2011 Draft (#91 overall)

YEAR	TEAM	LVL	AGE	PA	R	2B	3B	HR	RBI	BB	K	SB	CS	AVG/OBP/SLG
2019	ELP	AAA	29	113	17	5	1	5	20	14	18	0	0	.372/.469/.606
2019	SF	MLB	29	171	28	13	3	6	26	13	35	1	1	.290/.351/.529
2019	SD	MLB	29	19	1	0	0	0	2	0	7	0	0	.158/.158/.158
2020	SF	MLB	30	170	28	10	1	10	27	16	30	0	0	.298/.371/.576
2021 FS	SF	MLB	31	600	82	30	5	21	82	52	123	4	2	.265/.340/.461
2021 DC	SF	MLB	31	423	58	21	3	15	57	36	87	2	2	.265/.340/.461

Comparables: Rondell White, Jason Kubel, Marty Cordova

After a mostly-uneventful career that alternated between bench player and injured player, A-Dick managed to pack enough drama into the past September to make up for lost time. On the first day of the month, he took full advantage of Coors Field, blasting three homers and notching six RBI in a five-hit outing (all career highs, of course). Almost two weeks later, he returned a false positive on a COVID-19 test, causing a cancelled game, fears for the team's schedule and concerns for his pregnant wife Jennifer. All's well that ends well, and September concluded with a healthy and hitting Dickerson and a new member of the family, as Jennifer delivered Levi on the 24th. Dickerson showed enough on the field to earn a look for a strong-side, corner outfield platoon spot in 2021. He'll hope to provide plenty of power and on-base ability—this time with none of the past September's drama.

YEAR	TEAM	LVL	AGE	PA	DRC+	BABIP	BRR	FRAA	WARP
2019	ELP	AAA	29	113	125	.417	0.6	1B(6): -0.5, LF(6): 0.3, RF(3): 0.1	0.7
2019	SF	MLB	29	171	103	.339	0.5	LF(44): -4.5, RF(1): -0.2	0.1
2019	SD	MLB	29	19	67	.250	0.2	LF(6): -0.1	0.0
2020	SF	MLB	30	170	128	.312	-0.1	LF(41): -0.3, RF(5): 0.7	0.8
2021 FS	SF	MLB	31	600	121	.306	0.0	LF -1, 1B 0	3.0
2021 DC	SF	MLB	31	423	121	.306	0.0	LF -1	2.1

Steven Duggar RF

Born: 11/04/93   Age: 27   Bats: L   Throws: R
Height: 6'1"   Weight: 187   Origin: Round 6, 2015 Draft (#186 overall)

YEAR	TEAM	LVL	AGE	PA	R	2B	3B	HR	RBI	BB	K	SB	CS	AVG/OBP/SLG
2018	SAC	AAA	24	356	52	27	4	4	21	39	103	11	4	.272/.354/.421
2018	SF	MLB	24	152	20	11	1	2	17	10	44	5	1	.255/.303/.390
2019	SAC	AAA	25	102	24	6	1	3	13	18	21	2	3	.337/.461/.542
2019	SF	MLB	25	281	26	12	2	4	28	16	78	1	4	.234/.278/.341
2020	SF	MLB	26	36	3	2	0	0	3	1	11	1	0	.176/.222/.235
2021 FS	SF	MLB	27	600	66	24	5	11	57	54	183	7	4	.221/.297/.350
2021 DC	SF	MLB	27	126	13	5	1	2	12	11	38	1	1	.221/.297/.350

Comparables: Chad Hermansen, Laynce Nix, Luis Terrero

Not to be confused with the Diggers, a far-left Haight-Ashbury commune from the '60s, Duggar's Summer of Love was really only a couple of months as the starting center fielder in 2019. Since then, it's been too many bad trips to the plate, and he may be far out of the Giants' plans now.

YEAR	TEAM	LVL	AGE	PA	DRC+	BABIP	BRR	FRAA	WARP
2018	SAC	AAA	24	356	103	.392	-0.1	CF(74): 9.6	1.9
2018	SF	MLB	24	152	70	.354	3.6	CF(40): -3.4	0.0
2019	SAC	AAA	25	102	138	.424	0.2	CF(19): 0.4	0.9
2019	SF	MLB	25	281	61	.313	-1.4	CF(39): 2.1, RF(34): -0.8	-0.6
2020	SF	MLB	26	36	68	.261	-0.8	LF(11): 0.4, RF(7): -0.3, CF(4): -0.3	-0.2
2021 FS	SF	MLB	27	600	79	.312	0.6	LF 5, CF 1	0.7
2021 DC	SF	MLB	27	126	79	.312	0.1	LF 1, CF 0	0.1

Jae-Gyun Hwang 황재균 3B
Born: 07/28/87 Age: 33 Bats: R Throws: R
Height: 6'0" Weight: 215 Origin:

YEAR	TEAM	LVL	AGE	PA	R	2B	3B	HR	RBI	BB	K	SB	CS	AVG/OBP/SLG
2018	KT	KBO	30	588	76	41	3	25	88	49	120	14	7	.296/.358/.526
2019	KT	KBO	31	507	78	16	3	20	67	52	71	10	7	.283/.357/.467
2020	KT	KBO	32	600	108	35	5	21	97	47	98	11	6	.312/.370/.512
2021								No projection						

As Willie Bloomquist embodied the replacement-level big leaguer, Hwang is kind of a litmus test for any Korean who dreams of playing stateside. In the KBO, Hwang is among the 15 best position players in the league, a durable third baseman and a star on offense and defense. He's not quite an MVP candidate, but Hwang's power, arm strength, soft hands, and general athleticism make him stand out in a circuit where popups are often an adventure and benches overflow with players who could never hack it in Rookie ball. When San Francisco took a chance on him in 2017 though, Hwang barely clung to the Giants' 40-man roster. He was an average hitter in Triple-A, and while he got a midsummer cup of coffee, the Giants declined to take a longer look while they played out the string in September. That's no knock on Hwang; big leaguers are just really, really freaking good.

YEAR	TEAM	LVL	AGE	PA	DRC+	BABIP	BRR	FRAA	WARP
2018	KT	KBO	30	588					
2019	KT	KBO	31	507					
2020	KT	KBO	32	600					
2021					No projection				

Jin-De Jhang 張進德 C
Born: 05/17/93 Age: 28 Bats: L Throws: R
Height: 5'9" Weight: 225 Origin:

YEAR	TEAM	LVL	AGE	PA	R	2B	3B	HR	RBI	BB	K	SB	CS	AVG/OBP/SLG
2018	ALT	AA	25	135	13	8	0	1	23	11	14	0	0	.320/.373/.410
2019	GIB	ROK	26	50	5	1	1	1	7	6	4	1	0	.256/.340/.395
2019	RIC	AA	26	100	1	1	0	1	7	6	15	0	0	.138/.190/.181
2020	FUB	CPBL	27	321	49	22	0	14	47	28	30	2	2	.375/.429/.595
2021 FS	SF	MLB	28	600	52	26	2	10	56	34	102	0	1	.236/.284/.349

Comparables: Jhonatan Solano, Manny Piña, Francisco Arcia

Signed by the Pittsburgh Pirates in 2011 from Taiwan, Jhang spent much of the decade in their system, reaching Triple-A. Regarded as a solid defender behind the plate by prospect evaluators–backed up by his +12 FRAA across his MiLB career–Jhang had a journeyman backup catcher career path in front of him before injuries began to cut into his playing time. After spending a year in the Giants' system in 2019, he went back to Taiwan, entered the 2020 CPBL Draft, and signed with the Guardians. Marking his July 25 debut with a pair of doubles, Jhang provided the anemic Guardians' offense with a much-needed jolt in the second half of the season.

YEAR	TEAM	P. COUNT	FRM RUNS	BLK RUNS	THRW RUNS	TOT RUNS
2018	ALT	2990	1.8	0.0	-0.3	1.5
2019	RIC	3129	2.8	0.0	0.8	3.5
2021	SF	16650	5.5	-0.1	0.2	5.6
2021	SF	16650	5.5	1.0	0.2	6.7

YEAR	TEAM	LVL	AGE	PA	DRC+	BABIP	BRR	FRAA	WARP
2018	ALT	AA	25	135	123	.352	-0.3	C(22): 1.9	0.8
2019	GIB	ROK	26	50		.256			
2019	RIC	AA	26	100	41	.154	-0.4	C(26): 4.2	0.3
2020	FUB	CPBL	27	321		.385			
2021 FS	SF	MLB	28	600	74	.271	-0.7	C7	1.1

Marco Luciano SS
Born: 09/10/01   Age: 19   Bats: R   Throws: R
Height: 6'2"   Weight: 178   Origin: International Free Agent, 2018

YEAR	TEAM	LVL	AGE	PA	R	2B	3B	HR	RBI	BB	K	SB	CS	AVG/OBP/SLG
2019	GIO	ROK	17	178	46	9	2	10	38	27	39	8	6	.322/.438/.616
2019	SK	SS	17	38	6	4	0	0	4	5	6	1	0	.212/.316/.333
2021 FS	SF	MLB	19	600	45	21	3	7	48	41	198	11	6	.192/.253/.286

Comparables: Sergio Alcántara, Jonathan Araúz, Hanser Alberto

Whether it's responsible or not to base a player's comment off of a video from a fall instructional league game will be a matter for historians. But, absent a trove of 2020 data on the Giants' top prospect, we were left with one scene from early November: a static, centerfield video of Luciano absolutely cranking a fastball from Rockies lefty Ryan Rolison with a 119 mph EV bomb to the pull side. Among major-league hitters in 2020, the only player to top this exit velocity was Giancarlo Stanton. Though we only have a center-field view, Giants coach Matt Daniels tweeted that it was "quite possibly the furthest [sic] home run I've ever witnessed in person." For good measure, Luciano executed an exasperated hurl of a bat flip, as if disgusted that pitcher and ball had the hubris to even hope for success. Luciano still has a bit of a journey to Oracle Park, but his legend has already landed at SFO, taken BART into the city, grabbed a Tesora from Philz Coffee and now waits expectantly at 24 Willie Mays Plaza for his owner to claim him.

YEAR	TEAM	LVL	AGE	PA	DRC+	BABIP	BRR	FRAA	WARP
2019	GIO	ROK	17	178		.378			
2019	SK	SS	17	38	96	.259	-0.2	SS(9): -0.8	0.0
2021 FS	SF	MLB	19	600	48	.283	1.1	SS 3	-1.8

Luis Matos OF
Born: 01/28/02 Age: 19 Bats: R Throws: R
Height: 5'11" Weight: 160 Origin: International Free Agent, 2018

YEAR	TEAM	LVL	AGE	PA	R	2B	3B	HR	RBI	BB	K	SB	CS	AVG/OBP/SLG
2019	GIO	ROK	17	20	5	1	0	0	1	1	1	1	1	.438/.550/.500
2019	DSL GIA	ROK	17	270	60	24	2	7	47	19	30	20	2	.362/.430/.570
2021 FS	SF	MLB	19	600	45	18	3	8	49	29	188	35	7	.198/.248/.289

Comparables: Alex Verdugo, Victor Robles, Luis Arraez

A 2019 July 2nd signing from Venezuela, Matos is still in that blessed dreamland where the tools could become anything: elite batting average, plate discipline, surprising power upside, lightning speed, the defense to stick in center field. Anything seldom becomes everything, but there should be at least a couple of somethings in Matos' future.

YEAR	TEAM	LVL	AGE	PA	DRC+	BABIP	BRR	FRAA	WARP
2019	GIO	ROK	17	20		.467			
2019	DSL GIA	ROK	17	270		.386			
2021 FS	SF	MLB	19	600	47	.281	3.7	CF -4	-2.2

Hunter Pence RF

Born: 04/13/83   Age: 38   Bats: R   Throws: R
Height: 6'4"   Weight: 216   Origin: Round 2, 2004 Draft (#64 overall)

YEAR	TEAM	LVL	AGE	PA	R	2B	3B	HR	RBI	BB	K	SB	CS	AVG/OBP/SLG
2018	SAC	AAA	35	111	11	4	0	1	13	6	24	0	0	.301/.342/.369
2018	SF	MLB	35	248	19	11	1	4	24	11	59	5	1	.226/.258/.332
2019	TEX	MLB	36	316	53	17	1	18	59	26	69	6	1	.297/.358/.552
2020	SF	MLB	37	56	4	0	1	2	6	3	15	0	0	.096/.161/.250
2021 FS	*SF*	*MLB*	*38*	*600*	*59*	*23*	*1*	*17*	*65*	*43*	*159*	*5*	*2*	*.233/.293/.375*

Comparables: Jason Lane, Brian Jordan, Ruben Sierra

Of the four stops on Pence's résumé, San Francisco saw his most successful run and became his spiritual home. Arriving in 2012, just in time for the second of the Giants' three titles, Pence instantly became a middle-of-the-order bat, reliable everyday right fielder and a scooter-riding, coffee-loving, fan-engaging free spirit beloved of the Bay's aging hippies and tech bros alike. After an improbable 2019 fountain-of-youth rejuvenation in Arlington, Pence returned to play his swan song in Oracle Park—but, sadly, only the cardboard fans were there to hear it. While it would have been nice for Pence to receive a proper send-off, Giants fans will remember the giddy, buzzing, glory years of the early teens, not the feeble valediction that ended, in August, the career of one of the most distinctive and likable players of the current century.

YEAR	TEAM	LVL	AGE	PA	DRC+	BABIP	BRR	FRAA	WARP
2018	SAC	AAA	35	111	94	.380	-0.1	RF(12): 0.1, LF(11): 0.2	0.1
2018	SF	MLB	35	248	66	.282	0.4	LF(44): -3.1, RF(12): -1.2	-0.8
2019	TEX	MLB	36	316	121	.333	0.9	LF(16): 1.1, RF(8): 0.1	1.7
2020	SF	MLB	37	56	68	.086	0.1	LF(5): 0.2, RF(5): -0.0	-0.1
2021 FS	*SF*	*MLB*	*38*	*600*	*85*	*.296*	*-0.3*	*LF 2, RF 1*	*0.5*

Buster Posey C

Born: 03/27/87   Age: 34   Bats: R   Throws: R
Height: 6'1"   Weight: 213   Origin: Round 1, 2008 Draft (#5 overall)

YEAR	TEAM	LVL	AGE	PA	R	2B	3B	HR	RBI	BB	K	SB	CS	AVG/OBP/SLG
2018	SF	MLB	31	448	47	22	1	5	41	45	53	3	2	.284/.359/.382
2019	SF	MLB	32	445	43	24	0	7	38	34	71	0	0	.257/.320/.368
2021 FS	*SF*	*MLB*	*34*	*600*	*70*	*25*	*1*	*12*	*69*	*60*	*89*	*4*	*2*	*.263/.343/.388*
2021 DC	*SF*	*MLB*	*34*	*412*	*48*	*17*	*1*	*8*	*47*	*41*	*61*	*3*	*1*	*.263/.343/.388*

Comparables: Johnny Bench, Gary Carter, Brian McCann

As a likely Hall-of-Famer and most significant remaining link to the Giants' championship era, Posey has earned the privilege of directing the last act of his playing career as he sees fit. Fortunately for Farhan Zaidi, whatever the franchise cornerstone

YEAR	TEAM	P. COUNT	FRM RUNS	BLK RUNS	THRW RUNS	TOT RUNS
2018	SF	12351	0.9	0.7	0.1	1.7
2019	SF	13868	10.1	2.2	1.6	13.8
2021	SF	9620	3.6	0.8	0.8	5.3
2021	SF	9620	3.6	1.7	0.8	6.2

wants is likely to dovetail with current organizational aspirations. Posey should be fully healthy after opting out of 2020 (so he could visit his newly adopted twin daughters, who had to spend time in the neonatal intensive care unit), returning in 2021 to his age-34 season and the final guaranteed year on his contract (with a team option in 2022). While it's difficult to tell whether the decline in his bat (just look at the DRC+ plummet since 2017) is due to persistent injury or the inevitability of skills erosion after a decade of full-time catching in the majors, Posey's defense has remained solidly above average. With Bart now ready to try his hand against major-league competition, Posey has a chance to share the load at backstop, possibly cycling to first base a time or two a week (though an NL designated hitter would obviously benefit Posey more than most). One of two paths seems likely for Posey in the coming season: a healthy callback to his previous, younger excellence—thereby letting Bart gain reps in Triple-A—or an on-the-job mentorship of his eventual successor at the big-league level. Either of these outcomes would suit the rebuilding Giants just fine.

YEAR	TEAM	LVL	AGE	PA	DRC+	BABIP	BRR	FRAA	WARP
2018	SF	MLB	31	448	106	.316	-1.3	C(88): 0.1, 1B(13): 1.5	2.4
2019	SF	MLB	32	445	85	.296	-1.4	C(101): 14.9, 1B(4): -0.1	2.7
2021 FS	SF	MLB	34	600	106	.295	-0.6	C 6, 1B 1	3.5
2021 DC	SF	MLB	34	412	106	.295	-0.4	C 5, 1B 1	2.3

Casey Schmitt 3B
Born: 03/01/99 Age: 22 Bats: R Throws: R
Height: 6'2" Weight: 200 Origin: Round 2, 2020 Draft (#49 overall)

Despite having both pitching and hitting success as a two-way player at San Diego State, the Giants' third-round pick Schmitt is more Jared Walsh than Shohei Ohtani. Oh, you didn't know Walsh tried his hand at pitching for a while? Exactly.

Luis Toribio 3B

Born: 09/28/00 Age: 20 Bats: L Throws: R
Height: 6'1" Weight: 165 Origin: International Free Agent, 2017

YEAR	TEAM	LVL	AGE	PA	R	2B	3B	HR	RBI	BB	K	SB	CS	AVG/OBP/SLG
2018	DSL GIA	ROK	17	274	44	13	1	10	39	51	62	4	1	.270/.423/.479
2019	GIO	ROK	18	234	45	15	3	3	33	45	54	4	5	.297/.436/.459
2019	SK	SS	18	13	2	1	0	0	0	2	5	0	0	.273/.385/.364
2021 FS	SF	MLB	20	600	45	20	3	7	47	50	224	3	2	.180/.254/.273

Comparables: Austin Riley, Ryan McMahon, Sherten Apostel

Evan Longoria's seemingly interminable contract (remember how mad people got about that?) finally ends after 2022, and the Giants hope Toribio can step in around then to take over the hot corner and be the middle-of-the-order power bat that Longoria stopped being even before he made his way from one Bay to the other.

YEAR	TEAM	LVL	AGE	PA	DRC+	BABIP	BRR	FRAA	WARP
2018	DSL GIA	ROK	17	274		.333			
2019	GIO	ROK	18	234		.400			
2019	SK	SS	18	13	105	.500	-1.4	3B(3): -0.6	-0.2
2021 FS	SF	MLB	20	600	46	.289	0.0	3B -6	-3.7

LaMonte Wade Jr LF

Born: 01/01/94 Age: 27 Bats: L Throws: L
Height: 6'1" Weight: 205 Origin: Round 9, 2015 Draft (#260 overall)

YEAR	TEAM	LVL	AGE	PA	R	2B	3B	HR	RBI	BB	K	SB	CS	AVG/OBP/SLG
2018	CHA	AA	24	201	30	2	1	7	27	26	20	5	2	.298/.393/.444
2018	ROC	AAA	24	294	24	9	3	4	21	38	54	5	1	.229/.337/.336
2019	ROC	AAA	25	334	47	12	1	5	24	56	48	7	2	.246/.392/.356
2019	MIN	MLB	25	69	10	2	1	2	5	11	9	0	1	.196/.348/.375
2020	MIN	MLB	26	44	3	3	0	0	1	4	9	1	1	.231/.318/.308
2021 FS	SF	MLB	27	600	72	26	3	12	62	71	121	1	1	.244/.345/.382
2021 DC	SF	MLB	27	97	11	4	0	2	10	11	19	0	0	.244/.345/.382

Comparables: César Puello, Shin-Soo Choo, Gabe Gross

You might say that LaMonte wade-d into the Twins lineup after a mid-August injury to Byron Buxton. He found the waters deep and choppy though, and will likely spend 2021 bobbing between Rochester and Minneapolis.

YEAR	TEAM	LVL	AGE	PA	DRC+	BABIP	BRR	FRAA	WARP
2018	CHA	AA	24	201	141	.301	1.5	LF(25): 1.1, CF(10): 1.1, RF(8): -0.2	1.3
2018	ROC	AAA	24	294	97	.277	0.2	LF(58): 2.8, RF(16): 0.5	0.5
2019	ROC	AAA	25	334	106	.280	0.8	RF(34): -6.5, LF(28): -1.4, CF(11): -1.0	0.3
2019	MIN	MLB	25	69	104	.200	0.0	CF(14): 0.9, LF(8): -0.6, RF(6): -0.7	0.2
2020	MIN	MLB	26	44	88	.300	0.1	1B(4): -0.1, CF(4): -0.2, LF(3): -0.3	-0.1
2021 FS	SF	MLB	27	600	105	.296	-0.5	RF 0, LF 1	1.9
2021 DC	SF	MLB	27	97	105	.296	-0.1	RF 0, LF 0	0.3

Will Wilson SS

Born: 07/21/98 Age: 22 Bats: R Throws: R
Height: 6'0" Weight: 184 Origin: Round 1, 2019 Draft (#15 overall)

YEAR	TEAM	LVL	AGE	PA	R	2B	3B	HR	RBI	BB	K	SB	CS	AVG/OBP/SLG
2019	ORM	ROK+	20	200	23	10	3	5	18	14	47	0	0	.281/.335/.449
2021 FS	SF	MLB	22	600	43	19	3	8	48	32	204	0	1	.188/.237/.281

In a trade that was entirely emblematic of both Farhan Zaidi's approach to talent acquisition and the financial landscape of 2020 baseball at large, Wilson, an Angels first-round pick from 2019, was essentially purchased by the Giants for the cost of Zack Cozart's contract. It was unlikely the injured Cozart would ever play for the Giants, and he in fact did not, as he was released well before spring training even began. Wilson's hopes remain higher: he is a polished college bat, albeit one with strikeout and groundball proclivities. After some seasoning in the upper-minors, he could slot into second or third base, even if he may not have the glove to be Brandon Crawford's heir apparent at shortstop. Will he be worth it? Chances are, we'll see Wilson soon enough to know. Say that three times fast.

YEAR	TEAM	LVL	AGE	PA	DRC+	BABIP	BRR	FRAA	WARP
2019	ORM	ROK+	20	200		.353			
2021 FS	SF	MLB	22	600	41	.278	-0.2		-2.8

San Francisco Giants 2021

Melvin Adon RHP
Born: 06/09/94   Age: 27   Bats: L   Throws: R
Height: 6'3"   Weight: 246   Origin: International Free Agent, 2015

YEAR	TEAM	LVL	AGE	W	L	SV	G	GS	IP	H	HR	BB/9	K/9	K	GB%	BABIP
2018	SJ	HI-A	24	2	5	0	16	15	77^2	82	6	3.9	8.2	71	53.7%	.342
2019	RIC	AA	25	2	6	14	36	0	45	38	2	5.2	11.8	59	50.5%	.360
2019	SAC	AAA	25	0	1	0	12	0	10^1	16	1	7.0	15.7	18	50.0%	.517
2021 FS	SF	MLB	27	2	2	0	57	0	50	44	6	5.0	9.2	50	45.7%	.285

Comparables: Vicente Campos, Gonzalez Germen, James Marvel

If you have triple-digit heat but no idea where it's going, you might be less a pitcher than a threat to public safety. Unfortunately for Melvin Adon (but perhaps not for batters, catchers, umpires and proximate bystanders), an unspecified arm injury in the Dominican Winter League may silence the sirens for the time being.

YEAR	TEAM	LVL	AGE	WHIP	ERA	DRA-	WARP	MPH	FB%	WHF	CSP
2018	SJ	HI-A	24	1.49	4.87	116	-0.4				
2019	RIC	AA	25	1.42	2.60	103	-0.2				
2019	SAC	AAA	25	2.32	13.94	106	0.1				
2021 FS	SF	MLB	27	1.46	4.37	104	0.1				

Tyler Beede RHP
Born: 05/23/93   Age: 28   Bats: R   Throws: R
Height: 6'2"   Weight: 216   Origin: Round 1, 2014 Draft (#14 overall)

YEAR	TEAM	LVL	AGE	W	L	SV	G	GS	IP	H	HR	BB/9	K/9	K	GB%	BABIP
2018	SAC	AAA	25	4	9	0	33	10	74	82	10	6.8	9.1	75	39.0%	.353
2018	SF	MLB	25	0	1	0	2	2	7^2	9	0	9.4	10.6	9	45.5%	.409
2019	SAC	AAA	26	2	2	0	7	7	34^2	24	3	3.6	12.7	49	33.8%	.300
2019	SF	MLB	26	5	10	0	24	22	117	127	22	3.5	8.7	113	44.0%	.312
2021 FS	SF	MLB	28	9	9	0	26	26	150	140	21	4.3	9.5	158	43.1%	.295
2021 DC	SF	MLB	28	5	4	0	38	8	62.3	58	9	4.3	9.5	65	43.1%	.295

Comparables: Joe Ross, Clay Holmes, Rookie Davis

When we last saw Beede on a mound, he was perhaps the most consistent starter in the tail-end of the Giants' 2019 season. Following a 2020 lost to Tommy John rehab, the Giants are counting on a healthy Beede to pick up where he left off—as a mid-rotation starter with upside for more. How might he achieve that ever-elusive "more"? He might consider going away from his bread-and-butter four-seamer, as it didn't fool major-league hitters during his up-and-down 2019. Add "refining pitch mix" to the to-do list, too, along with the inevitable rehab steps that will keep Beede from a major-league mound until sometime in the middle of the 2021 season.

YEAR	TEAM	LVL	AGE	WHIP	ERA	DRA-	WARP	MPH	FB%	WHF	CSP
2018	SAC	AAA	25	1.86	7.05	108	0.3				
2018	SF	MLB	25	2.22	8.22	94	0.1	94.3	51.8%	30.6%	
2019	SAC	AAA	26	1.10	2.34	49	1.4				
2019	SF	MLB	26	1.48	5.08	107	0.7	96.0	56.2%	26.2%	
2021 FS	SF	MLB	28	1.42	4.42	104	1.1	95.9	56.0%	26.4%	45.2%
2021 DC	SF	MLB	28	1.42	4.42	104	0.4	95.9	56.0%	26.4%	45.2%

John Brebbia RHP

Born: 05/30/90 Age: 31 Bats: L Throws: R
Height: 6'1" Weight: 200 Origin: Round 30, 2011 Draft (#929 overall)

YEAR	TEAM	LVL	AGE	W	L	SV	G	GS	IP	H	HR	BB/9	K/9	K	GB%	BABIP
2018	MEM	AAA	28	2	0	2	11	0	13^2	16	3	2.6	15.8	24	6.1%	.433
2018	STL	MLB	28	3	3	2	45	0	50^2	43	5	2.8	10.7	60	32.3%	.299
2019	STL	MLB	29	3	4	0	66	0	72^2	59	6	3.3	10.8	87	27.8%	.293
2021 FS	SF	MLB	31	2	2	0	57	0	50	42	8	2.4	10.1	55	30.1%	.270
2021 DC	SF	MLB	31	0	0	0	19	0	19.3	16	3	2.4	10.1	21	30.1%	.270

Comparables: Hansel Robles, Nick Wittgren, Emilio Pagán

Brebbia has already overcome a 30th-round draft slot, release from the Yankees, two years in independent ball and a serious case of chia beard to carve out a bullpen career, so Tommy John surgery should just be a speed bump for him. The Giants signed him over the winter, banking on him making a full recovery.

YEAR	TEAM	LVL	AGE	WHIP	ERA	DRA-	WARP	MPH	FB%	WHF	CSP
2018	MEM	AAA	28	1.46	4.61	29	0.6				
2018	STL	MLB	28	1.16	3.20	65	1.2	96.7	53.2%	29.6%	
2019	STL	MLB	29	1.18	3.59	83	1.0	95.5	56.6%	29.0%	
2021 FS	SF	MLB	31	1.10	3.21	84	0.7	95.8	55.7%	29.2%	49.5%
2021 DC	SF	MLB	31	1.10	3.21	84	0.3	95.8	55.7%	29.2%	49.5%

Seth Corry LHP
Born: 11/03/98 Age: 22 Bats: L Throws: L
Height: 6'2" Weight: 195 Origin: Round 3, 2017 Draft (#96 overall)

YEAR	TEAM	LVL	AGE	W	L	SV	G	GS	IP	H	HR	BB/9	K/9	K	GB%	BABIP
2018	GIO	ROK	19	3	1	0	9	9	38	38	1	4.0	9.9	42	42.6%	.352
2018	SK	SS	19	1	2	0	5	5	19²	14	1	6.9	7.8	17	51.9%	.245
2019	AUG	LO-A	20	9	3	0	27	26	122²	73	4	4.3	12.6	172	43.2%	.272
2021 FS	SF	MLB	22	2	3	0	57	0	50	45	7	7.0	9.6	53	40.7%	.292

Comparables: Brailyn Marquez, Huascar Ynoa, Johan Oviedo

Corry is precisely the type of pop-up prospect it would have been particularly informative to see in 2020. The Utah high school draftee was barely a whisper on prospect lists until he ran roughshod over the Sally League in 2019, though his strikeout dominance and batted-ball luck covered for some spotty control. The velocity foundation is there for a mid-rotation lefty; it would have been nice to spend 2020 tracking the progression of his secondaries and the refinement of his mechanics. Alas. we'll have to wait a little longer to see if his breakout was a sustainable developmental leap or something else.

YEAR	TEAM	LVL	AGE	WHIP	ERA	DRA-	WARP	MPH	FB%	WHF	CSP
2018	GIO	ROK	19	1.45	2.61						
2018	SK	SS	19	1.47	5.49	300	-2.2				
2019	AUG	LO-A	20	1.07	1.76	68	2.7				
2021 FS	SF	MLB	22	1.69	5.60	122	-0.4				

Rico Garcia RHP
Born: 01/10/94 Age: 27 Bats: R Throws: R
Height: 5'9" Weight: 201 Origin: Round 30, 2016 Draft (#890 overall)

YEAR	TEAM	LVL	AGE	W	L	SV	G	GS	IP	H	HR	BB/9	K/9	K	GB%	BABIP
2018	LAN	HI-A	24	7	7	0	16	15	100	99	12	2.0	9.1	101	45.1%	.316
2018	HFD	AA	24	6	2	0	11	11	67	54	8	2.7	8.2	61	43.4%	.266
2019	HFD	AA	25	8	2	0	13	13	68	41	4	3.0	11.5	87	47.3%	.261
2019	ABQ	AAA	25	2	4	0	13	13	61¹	77	14	4.1	7.5	51	35.6%	.335
2019	COL	MLB	25	0	1	0	2	1	6	9	3	7.5	3.0	2	39.1%	.300
2020	SF	MLB	26	1	1	0	12	0	10	13	1	3.6	6.3	7	45.5%	.375
2021 FS	SF	MLB	27	2	3	0	57	0	50	49	7	4.1	8.2	45	41.2%	.292

Comparables: Chase De Jong, Keury Mella, Sean Poppen

"It's not an excuse; it's an explanation" is a good way for a pitcher to justify bad Coors Field performances. After a move to Oracle Park, Garcia found that his former home wasn't done with him: half his earned-run output for the season came during a three-run September blowup in Denver. Rocky Mountain high, indeed.

YEAR	TEAM	LVL	AGE	WHIP	ERA	DRA-	WARP	MPH	FB%	WHF	CSP
2018	LAN	HI-A	24	1.21	3.42	85	1.2				
2018	HFD	AA	24	1.10	2.28	89	0.9				
2019	HFD	AA	25	0.94	1.85	60	1.7				
2019	ABQ	AAA	25	1.71	6.90	122	0.5				
2019	COL	MLB	25	2.33	10.50	149	-0.1	93.3	61.6%	16.2%	
2020	SF	MLB	26	1.70	5.40	104	0.1	97.3	56.5%	22.4%	
2021 FS	SF	MLB	27	1.44	4.60	109	0.0	96.2	57.9%	20.7%	44.6%

Sean Hjelle RHP

Born: 05/07/97 Age: 24 Bats: R Throws: R
Height: 6'11" Weight: 228 Origin: Round 2, 2018 Draft (#45 overall)

YEAR	TEAM	LVL	AGE	W	L	SV	G	GS	IP	H	HR	BB/9	K/9	K	GB%	BABIP
2018	SK	SS	21	0	0	0	12	12	21^1	24	4	1.7	9.3	22	49.3%	.317
2019	AUG	LO-A	22	1	2	0	9	9	40^2	41	3	2.0	9.7	44	62.4%	.336
2019	SJ	HI-A	22	5	5	0	14	14	77^2	73	2	2.2	8.5	73	65.5%	.329
2019	RIC	AA	22	1	2	0	5	5	25^1	38	1	3.2	7.5	21	47.1%	.430
2021 FS	SF	MLB	24	2	2	0	57	0	50	48	7	3.4	7.3	40	43.0%	.283

Comparables: Beau Burrows, Jeremy Bleich, Braden Shipley

Two things about Hjelle: he's 6-foot-11 and his last name is pronounced like the preserved fruit spread, or the colloquialism of "jealous." You'd be *jelly* of his height on a basketball court, but you'd probably trade a few inches for a few ticks on the heater if you were building the next Giant ace.

YEAR	TEAM	LVL	AGE	WHIP	ERA	DRA-	WARP	MPH	FB%	WHF	CSP
2018	SK	SS	21	1.31	5.06	212	-1.2				
2019	AUG	LO-A	22	1.23	2.66	109	-0.1				
2019	SJ	HI-A	22	1.18	2.78	84	0.9				
2019	RIC	AA	22	1.86	6.04	153	-0.8				
2021 FS	SF	MLB	24	1.35	4.34	103	0.1				

Casey Kelly RHP
Born: 10/04/89 Age: 31 Bats: R Throws: R
Height: 6'3" Weight: 215 Origin: Round 1, 2008 Draft (#30 overall)

YEAR	TEAM	LVL	AGE	W	L	SV	G	GS	IP	H	HR	BB/9	K/9	K	GB%	BABIP
2018	SAC	AAA	28	10	9	0	24	24	136	155	19	2.5	7.3	111	40.5%	.328
2018	SF	MLB	28	0	3	0	7	3	23²	28	3	1.9	6.1	16	50.0%	.316
2019	LG	KBO	29	14	12	0	29	29	180¹	164	7	2.0	6.3	126		
2020	LG	KBO	30	15	7	0	28	28	173¹	160	16	2.0	7.0	134		
2021									No projection							

Comparables: Jordan Lyles, Chris Stratton, Erasmo Ramírez

Kelly's comprehensive blandness has always made his game difficult to enjoy. Like Bon Iver, there's not any one flaw that stands out, but rather a collection of underwhelming traits and tools that leaves you wanting more. But while Kelly's stuff is a little light for MLB, it's plenty good in South Korea. He quickly emerged as LG's ace, and his collection of 45's on the scouting report made him one of the league's top starters. As with many other Quad-A talents, sometimes you just have to hit the road to find success.

YEAR	TEAM	LVL	AGE	WHIP	ERA	DRA-	WARP	MPH	FB%	WHF	CSP
2018	SAC	AAA	28	1.42	4.76	92	1.9				
2018	SF	MLB	28	1.39	3.04	78	0.5	93.6	52.7%	22.8%	
2019	LG	KBO	29	1.14	2.55						
2020	LG	KBO	30	1.15	3.32						
2021						No projection					

Reyes Moronta RHP
Born: 01/06/93 Age: 28 Bats: R Throws: R
Height: 5'10" Weight: 265 Origin: International Free Agent, 2011

YEAR	TEAM	LVL	AGE	W	L	SV	G	GS	IP	H	HR	BB/9	K/9	K	GB%	BABIP
2018	SF	MLB	25	5	2	1	69	0	65	34	4	5.1	10.9	79	42.5%	.213
2019	SF	MLB	26	3	7	0	56	0	56²	41	4	5.2	11.1	70	37.9%	.274
2021 FS	SF	MLB	28	2	2	13	57	0	50	39	5	5.1	11.3	62	39.1%	.286
2021 DC	SF	MLB	28	2	2	13	57	0	58	46	6	5.1	11.3	73	39.1%	.286

Comparables: José Leclerc, Keone Kela, Dan Altavilla

Given the carousel of failed closers that cycled through Gabe Kapler's bullpen in 2020, the job could very well be Moronta's to lose. The case for Moronta: high-90s heat combined with a diving slider. The challenge for Moronta: recovering from a Tommy John surgery, and perhaps picking up a little more command along the way.

YEAR	TEAM	LVL	AGE	WHIP	ERA	DRA-	WARP	MPH	FB%	WHF	CSP
2018	SF	MLB	25	1.09	2.49	69	1.4	98.4	51.0%	35.3%	
2019	SF	MLB	26	1.31	2.86	84	0.8	98.7	58.3%	29.4%	
2021 FS	SF	MLB	28	1.36	3.64	88	0.6	98.6	55.8%	31.4%	46.1%
2021 DC	SF	MLB	28	1.36	3.64	88	0.7	98.6	55.8%	31.4%	46.1%

Ricardo Pinto RHP

Born: 01/20/94 Age: 27 Bats: R Throws: R
Height: 6'0" Weight: 195 Origin:

YEAR	TEAM	LVL	AGE	W	L	SV	G	GS	IP	H	HR	BB/9	K/9	K	GB%	BABIP
2018	WS	HI-A	24	1	0	0	3	3	10²	13	2	6.8	6.8	8	52.8%	.324
2018	CHA	AAA	24	2	2	0	27	3	54¹	68	7	3.6	6.3	38	50.0%	.349
2019	MTG	AA	25	2	1	0	4	2	18²	20	2	3.9	7.2	15	22.8%	.333
2019	DUR	AAA	25	10	5	0	24	4	104²	96	18	4.0	8.3	96	48.0%	.283
2019	TB	MLB	25	0	0	0	2	0	2¹	4	1	7.7	0.0	0	45.5%	.300
2020	SK	KBO	26	6	15	0	30	30	162	198	19	5.0	6.2	112		
2021 FS	SF	MLB	27	2	3	0	57	0	50	49	7	4.1	7.4	40	43.1%	.288

Comparables: Chih-Wei Hu, Thyago Vieira, Miguel Almonte

Yikes. Former big leaguers are supposed to headline your rotation in the KBO, but in this case, the anchor was heavier than the ship. At one point in a dreadful stretch of 10 outings, he allowed four runs or more nine times, and his ERA in July and August was 8.95, a figure once thought to be only a theoretical possibility. You could chart Pinto's season by the shift in his facial reactions over the course of the year. Like a man navigating the stages of grief, spring smiles of disbelief soon gave way to visible frustration, then desperate pleas to the wind to push just one one of those soaring fly balls back into the yard. By early autumn, the collision of baseball and left field bleacher could do no more damage to Pinto's already cadaverous expression. As of this writing, he's still in the rotation, and his brow remains furrowed; the beatings will continue until morale improves.

YEAR	TEAM	LVL	AGE	WHIP	ERA	DRA-	WARP	MPH	FB%	WHF	CSP
2018	WS	HI-A	24	1.97	6.75	85	0.2				
2018	CHA	AAA	24	1.66	5.80	97	0.3				
2019	MTG	AA	25	1.50	4.82	130	-0.4				
2019	DUR	AAA	25	1.36	4.13	92	1.9				
2019	TB	MLB	25	2.57	15.43	135	0.0	97.1	66.7%	16.7%	
2020	SK	KBO	26	1.78	6.17						
2021 FS	SF	MLB	27	1.45	4.59	109	0.0	97.1	66.7%	16.7%	55.2%

San Francisco Giants 2021

Nick Swiney LHP
Born: 02/12/99   Age: 22   Bats: R   Throws: L
Height: 6'3"   Weight: 187   Origin: Round 2, 2020 Draft (#67 overall)

Do three wolves make a pack? Swiney joined fellow NC State products Will Wilson and Patrick Bailey in the Giants organization. He's a three-pitch lefty who will race his former teammates to see which canis lupus is the hungriest to get to the majors.

Giants Prospects

The State of the System:
The Giants' system is good, folks. There's no other way to say it. I know, it's weird to me too.

The Top Ten:

1. ★ ★ ★ *2021 Top 101 Prospect* **#8** ★ ★ ★

Marco Luciano SS   OFP: 70   ETA: Late 2022/2023
Born: 09/10/01   Age: 19   Bats: R   Throws: R   Height: 6'2"   Weight: 178
Origin: International Free Agent, 2018

The Report: Luciano has a hell of a swing. He takes lightning-fast cuts with a great bat path, producing loft and excellent bat speed. His bat-to-ball skills are solid given his age and how hard his move is to the ball. He's a strong young man, with plus power already and the potential for more. He has one of the highest offensive ceilings in baseball. There are some warts here, albeit the ones you would expect from a teenage hitting sensation. His plate approach is a bit aggressive; it's manifested more in weak contact than swing-and-miss so far, which bodes well for future adjustments, but he will have to make them. Defensively, he currently has the range and arm to play shortstop, though we wouldn't be surprised if he slides over to third if he loses a step as he gets older.

Development Track: Luciano hit an instructional league homer with a 119-mph exit velocity, per the @SFGProspects Twitter. He was at the alternate site and then fall instructs, and he held his own and then some against players who were way older. Luciano should make his full-season debut whenever full-season baseball returns, and we expect him to move pretty fast once he gets going.

Variance: High. Despite our optimism, he did just lose a bunch of game reps and has barely played outside the complex.

J.P. Breen's Fantasy Take: We're talking about a potential five-category contributor, and he could be a monster in four of those categories. Luciano is a top-15 dynasty prospect and a top-100 overall guy. Perhaps he slows down a bit and struggles to reach double-digit stolen bases; however, that's a minor quibble. All the normal caveats apply to the 19-year-old who has not yet played full-season ball, but he's one of the special ones.

San Francisco Giants 2021

─── ★ ★ ★ *2021 Top 101 Prospect* **#29** ★ ★ ★ ───

2 **Joey Bart C**   OFP: 60   ETA: Debuted in 2020
Born: 12/15/96   Age: 24   Bats: R   Throws: R   Height: 6'2"   Weight: 238
Origin: Round 1, 2018 Draft (#2 overall)

The Report: At the plate, Bart is at least above average. He's got decent pitch recognition and some power, which may fare very well with the fences moved in now at Oracle Park, but he still needs to work on polishing his hitting some more. He has a swing that can almost resemble a golf swing at times and really tries to attack low and middle of the zone pitches because of it. When he can get under a ball, he can really lift the ball up deep into the outfield. Behind the plate, though, he is a plus defender with a plus arm, often posting sub-2.0 pop times. When he's not trying to rush the throw, he can throw down to second with pinpoint accuracy. His framing has improved a fair amount and he seems more confident in that aspect of his defense.

Development Track: Bart started 2020 at the alternate site, but because of the Giants' catching situation after Buster Posey opted out of the season, Bart's missed time in 2019 because of freak hand injuries (a fractured left hand with High-A San Jose, a right thumb fracture in Arizona Fall League), and the everything about 2020, it seemed to be worth a shot to give Bart some regular playing time at the major league level. Making the jump from Double-A to MLB was not without the obvious struggles, but started to adjust as he got more reps in. Of course, with how short the season was, there wasn't necessarily enough time to really fully settle in if one is called up with only a little over a month left to play. It's clear that with more reps, his talent will truly show.

Variance: Medium. The hand injuries don't seem to be much of an issue but a lot depends on if he can harness his power as a hitter. Otherwise, do the bartman.

J.P. Breen's Fantasy Take: It's important to realize that 20-homer catchers don't grow on trees. The majors only had eight of them in 2019. Bart has the potential to reach the 25-homer plateau with 400-plus plate appearances, which would easily make him a top-10 catcher, even in disappointing years. I don't think he'll ever walk enough to be a Yasmani Grandal-type fantasy catcher; however, he should hit for more average.

─── ★ ★ ★ *2021 Top 101 Prospect* **#32** ★ ★ ★ ───

3 **Heliot Ramos CF**   OFP: 60   ETA: Late 2021/Early 2022
Born: 09/07/99   Age: 21   Bats: R   Throws: R   Height: 6'0"   Weight: 188
Origin: Round 1, 2017 Draft (#19 overall)

The Report: Ramos is a potential plus hit/plus power corner outfielder. The plus hit tool doesn't necessarily derive from above-average feel for contact—Ramos's power comes from some length, and swing-and-miss comes with it—but from the damage he can do when he does make contact. Ramos hits the ball hard, and he can hit it over the fence. He's a pretty good runner despite his somewhat square frame, and in an other than San Francisco's cavernous park, could play a bit of center field. He should be a good right fielder though, and the arm strength isn't an issue there.

Development Track: Ramos's season—such as it was—ended up bookended by oblique issues: one in Spring that would have delayed his start to the season, and one in the fall which cut short his time in instructs. This just continues his up and down prospect trajectory. 2020 was perhaps down a little due to the injuries and global pandemic limiting his ability to build off his strong 2019. A strong start to 2021 could find him in the Giants outfield mix quickly though. Some odd-year bullshit in the Bay Area would be refreshing at least.

Variance: Medium. Because of the oscillating arc of his development, Ramos has never really put together the kind of sustained, year-over-year performance that makes you completely confident that it's a plus corner outfield profile. That's a high offensive bar, but the tools are certainly there to vault it.

J.P. Breen's Fantasy Take: Ramos's long-term potential is something like Eloy Jimenez with less power. Ramos has better speed, of course, but he's already slowing down and only stole eight bases in 444 plate appearances in 2019. If everything comes good, Ramos is a 30-homer guy who hits .280 with 10 stolen bases. That's really damn good—Austin Meadows, circa 2019, good—but he carries significant volatility. His proximity to the big leagues puts him in the top-30 dynasty prospects.

─────── ★ ★ ★ *2021 Top 101 Prospect* **#75** ★ ★ ★ ───────

4
Hunter Bishop OF   OFP: 60   ETA: 2022
Born: 06/25/98   Age: 23   Bats: L   Throws: R   Height: 6'5"   Weight: 210
Origin: Round 1, 2019 Draft (#10 overall)

The Report: Like most of the class of 2019, attempting to rank Bishop based on such a small pro sample size is a difficult task. Reports out of Giants camp were all positive, especially with an emphasis on his defensive ability improving to the point he might stay in center field. His long strides and plus straight line speed play up in the gaps, it's a matter of getting the right reads of the bat. The athletic parts of his game are distinct even as he was labeled a "late bloomer" in college. The hit tool remains questionable until we see it against live pitching, but will note he fits the mold of the traditional high OBP/power corner outfielder.

Development Track: Playing center in San Francisco is no easy feat, with some of the biggest territory to cover this side of the Polo Grounds. If Bishop can make it work using his range, it only helps his overall outlook. The biggest area of development is simply proving he can handle high-quality offspeed in the upper levels of the minors.

Variance: Medium. There are a few finite qualities, like taking walks and hitting bombs, that seem to be inherent in nature that translate up and down whatever level being played at. Even if he's an average hitter, that likely gets you into all-star caliber territory.

J.P. Breen's Fantasy Take: Although defensive improvements are rarely celebrated in dynasty, they matter for Bishop. A defensive step forward puts less pressure on the development of his hit tool. We've all seen no-glove, low-average sluggers flame out after a year or two in the big leagues. Good-glove, low-average sluggers, however, can hold down everyday roles for years. The fact that Bishop can steal double-digit bases only enhances his dynasty value. I've really come around on Bishop over the past 12 months and now am fully on board with his being a fringe top-50 dynasty prospect. He's even more valuable in OBP leagues.

5 **Patrick Bailey** C   OFP: 55   ETA: 2023, 2022 if needed
Born: 05/29/99   Age: 22   Bats: S   Throws: R   Height: 6'2"   Weight: 207
Origin: Round 1, 2020 Draft (#13 overall)

The Report: Apparently the new market inefficiency is hoarding catchers. Bailey landed in the range of where many predicted he would be selected, although it came somewhat of a surprise hearing the Giants call his name. Unlike the NFL or NBA, you never draft for need in baseball with the amount of developmental and team fluctuations from year to year. Behind Buster Posey and Joey Bart, Bailey is a very solid catcher with the added value of being a switch-hitter with no real platoon weakness. There is nothing to his game that illuminates as a star quality, however, the sum of his tools project him as a starting backstop with some offensive upside.

Development Track: Maintaining a balanced work ethic between servicing your swing from both sides of the plate, while managing a pitching staff and game planning against an opponent, is perhaps the most difficult time management conundrum a professional player can endure. With the possibility he could be splitting time one day with Bart in the same lineup, alternating days between catching and first base, it might be worth doubly-focusing on the offensive output.

Variance: High. Catching is hard.

J.P. Breen's Fantasy Take: Bailey will either need to display impact in-game power potential or have a clear pathway to the big leagues before he's worth rostering in most dynasty formats. There are more interesting and higher-upside catchers in the minors if you insist on dipping your toes into the forbidden catching waters.

Will Wilson SS   OFP: 55   ETA: 2022
Born: 07/21/98   Age: 22   Bats: R   Throws: R   Height: 6'0"   Weight: 184
Origin: Round 1, 2019 Draft (#15 overall)

6. Will Wilson, SS

The Report: Wilson does a little bit of everything well. At the plate, his swing is smooth and balanced, with enough hand and wrist strength to get the barrel anywhere in the zone and drive the ball. He's got a well-built, mature frame that should generate average game power. He's an average runner that might slow down as he moves through his twenties, and that does make the defensive profile fit better at second base than shortstop. But he should be a sure-handed, solid enough defender there. This is a pretty dry recitation, but it's a pretty dry profile. It's also a major league one.

Development Track: As Keanan noted with Bishop, the 2019 draft class is difficult to deal with this year. Wilson is particularly tricky in that he doesn't have the loud tools of his organization mate. You want to see him hit at every level to stay confident he'll hit at the highest one. The lack of a carrying tool here means each individual one will have to scrape the projection for the OFP to become a reality.

Variance: Medium. Minimal pro track record, may lack a carrying tool, and could slide down the defensive spectrum.

J.P. Breen's Fantasy Take: Wilson is the ideal late-round pick in a supplemental draft, or the perfect last keeper. He's unexciting, but he's probably a big leaguer. He's the type of player that competitive dynasty teams have waiting in the wings or sitting in their MI slot. He's the type of boring 1.5-win player who's a fringe starter five years from now, who I'll be shamelessly defending on TINO as the perfect dynasty depth piece. Now that I'm writing this blurb, I'm surprised that I don't have Wilson on a single dynasty roster—I guess we'll have to change that soon.

7. Luis Matos OF   OFP: 55   ETA: 2024
Born: 01/28/02   Age: 19   Bats: R   Throws: R   Height: 5'11"   Weight: 160
Origin: International Free Agent, 2018

The Report: Signed as part of the Giants' rather loaded 2018 IFA class, Matos is a projectable, potential five-tool center fielder. The swing is advanced for his experience level, staying in the zone for a while, with good bat speed, and hinting at enough loft to tap into power as he fills out. His speed should keep him in center for the near future at least, and he's got a good shot to stick there as an above-average glove over the long term.

Development Track: Last year we told you to check back on Matos in four years. As it turns out though, we have to do prospect lists every year, so here we are. Matos looked good at instructs and while it would be an aggressive assignment, he could see full-season ball in 2021.

Variance: Extreme. He hasn't played significant games stateside. You can check back in three years now, but there's the potential the profile pops well before then. And anyway, there will be another list in 2022.

J.P. Breen's Fantasy Take: It's uncommon to find a teenager who is both a potential five-tool hitter and someone who isn't whiffing 25-plus percent of the time as a professional. Matos's plate discipline numbers suggest that he has a decent idea at the plate, and the tools are loud enough that he could be an impact guy in five years. The fact that he hasn't even seen full-season ball to this point is why Matos currently isn't a top-50 dynasty prospect. But he already ain't far off it.

8 Luis Toribio 3B   OFP: 55   ETA: 2024
Born: 09/28/00   Age: 20   Bats: L   Throws: R   Height: 6'1"   Weight: 165
Origin: International Free Agent, 2017

The Report: Signed for $300,000 while the Giants were in the penalty after inking Lucius Fox the previous summer, Toribio's bat has developed quickly as a pro. The stick was always going to be driving the profile, although the stout Toribio should be fine at third base. The hit and power tools are both potentially above-average and he's shown good plate discipline early in his pro career, albeit at levels where it's not all that hard to draw a walk.

Development Track: Toribio had alternate site and instructs time and should be well-situated for a full-season ball assignment in 2021 when we will get a better test of the offensive carrying tools.

Variance: Extreme. He hasn't played significant games stateside. You can check back in three years now, but there's the potential the profile pops well before then. And anyway, there will be another list in 2022.

J.P. Breen's Fantasy Take: Toribio doesn't have much physical projection remaining and won't be a threat on the basepaths, which puts all the pressure on his bat to carry his fantasy profile. He could be a power-average slugger. However, there's platoon risk and risk that he's simply been more physically developed than his peers in rookie ball. Toribio is a fringe top-200 dynasty prospect, though I have him a touch lower on my personal rankings list due to his age and how infrequently this type of fantasy profile translates to an impact big leaguer.

9 Alexander Canario CF   OFP: 55   ETA: 2024
Born: 05/07/00   Age: 21   Bats: R   Throws: R   Height: 6'1"   Weight: 165
Origin: International Free Agent, 2016

The Report: Canario's swing should go in the BP Prospect Team handbook as our dictionary definition of controlled violence. And it's just barely restrained, but it creates incredible bat speed and whippy loft that could generate big home run totals in the majors some day. It could also generate 200 strikeouts in Double-A. So you can probably guess the variance you will see below. Canario is an average runner better suited to right field than center, but he has the potential power to fit the corner outfield prospect mold.

Development Track: Canario's offensive profile was going to be more boom or bust than Toribio or even Matos, but man it would be a heckuva boom. There's an alternate history where he has a normal A-ball season this year and goes 110+ mph exit velo for 110+ mph exit velo with Luciano. Instead, his season ended with a dislocated shoulder and torn labrum during instructs. He's had shoulder surgery since and given the recovery time for that, the start of his 2021 might be in doubt.

Variance: Extreme. Take the copypasta from the two teenagers ahead of him on the list and add a significant shoulder injury. And given the effort in the swing, any erosion of the shoulder strength could be a big problem

J.P. Breen's Fantasy Take: I fully acknowledge the upside, but we're talking about a 20-year-old who hasn't yet played full-season ball and had a 32.4 percent strikeout rate at his most recent minor-league stop. Add in the shoulder surgery, and I've got nightmares of Gregory Polanco dancing through my head. Most lists have Canario as a top-100 dynasty prospect. He's much lower than that for me.

10 Seth Corry LHP   OFP: 50   ETA: 2022
Born: 11/03/98 Age: 22 Bats: L Throws: L Height: 6'2" Weight: 195
Origin: Round 3, 2017 Draft (#96 overall)

The Report: Corry spent 2019 dominating the South Atlantic League with a K/9 of 12.6. The lefty has a fastball he can dial up to 95 with good extension and deception. He also has a potentially above-average curve and change. The stuff is not in question, but control has been an issue for him throughout his pro career.

Development Track: Corry impressed at instructs with his above-average three pitch mix. He still struggles with walks, and improving his control will be the biggest developmental step for him moving forward as a potential starting pitcher.

Variance: High. Could be a back of the rotation guy if the stuff sticks/command is good, could be a reliever.

J.P. Breen's Fantasy Take: Until the control/command takes a massive step forward, you can feel free to remove Corry from your dynasty lists. Don't be enticed by the shiny A-ball ERA.

The Prospects You Meet Outside The Top Ten

MLB arms, but less upside than you'd like

Sean Hjelle RHP Born: 05/07/97 Age: 24 Bats: R Throws: R Height: 6'11" Weight: 228 Origin: Round 2, 2018 Draft (#45 overall)
Potentially one of the tallest major leaguers in history, the 6-foot-11 Hjelle drops his low-90s fastball off a metaphorical skyscraper on hitters and pairs it with a viable curve and change. The arsenal all grades out as average, but Hjelle bucks the usual tall pitcher issues—maybe he's too tall for them—with a repeatable

delivery and above-average command. He did get knocked around a bit in his brief 2019 Double-A appearances, but once he conquers the upper minors in 2021, he should be ready to be a number four starter in San Francisco by 2022.

Interesting 2020 draft follows

Casey Schmitt   3B   Born: 03/01/99   Age: 22   Bats: R   Throws: R   Height: 6'2"   Weight: 200   Origin: Round 2, 2020 Draft (#49 overall)
Schmitt does a little bit of everything. He was San Diego State's closer his first two years there, running his fastball into the mid-90s and pairing it with a potential above-average splitter. He was announced as a third baseman only though, and while he has the raw power for the hot corner, the pop never consistently showed up in games in the pitcher-friendly confines of his home park. That power comes with some wrap and length though, so although his track record with wood bats is all right, there might be some adjusting to do against pro arms.

Kyle Harrison   Born: 08/12/01   Age: 19   Bats: R   Throws: L   Height: 6'2"   Weight: 200   Origin: Round 3, 2020 Draft (#85 overall)
Taken in the third round by the Giants and given a first round bonus, and he's absolutely confounding as an overslot prep arm. We all have a picture of our head of what this profile looks like on the mound. The frame is about right, 6-foot-2 and 200 lbs, although perhaps that's less projection than you'd like. The fastball is more low-90s than mid-90s, the profile more pitchability than power stuff. There's even an advanced change for a prep. He's difficult to pigeonhole among the 2020 prep arm class, but he's a solid pitching prospect nonetheless.

MLB arms, but probably relievers

Conner Menez   LHP   Born: 05/29/95   Age: 26   Bats: L   Throws: L   Height: 6'2"   Weight: 206   Origin: Round 14, 2016 Draft (#425 overall)
Menez's 2020 stint with the Giants went better than his 2019 one on paper, but he continued to have some struggles with the long ball. His recently developed slider looks promising though, and gives him a second breaking ball look from the left side. He'd be assured of more major league time pre-three-batter-rule, but he could still be a useful reliever to deploy as is.

Dedniel Nunez   RHP   Born: 06/05/96   Age: 25   Bats: R   Throws: R   Height: 6'2"   Weight: 180   Origin: International Free Agent, 2016
Plucked out of the Mets org in December's Rule 5 draft, Nuñez has a high-spin fastball he can run up to 95—although it sits a few ticks lower—and a fringy slider and change. He's best suited to relief, but given that he's been a starter for most of his pro career and has three pitches, he could help out in a multi-inning stints or as the occasional bulk guy. Or he could get returned to Mets in March.

Top Talents 25 and Under (as of 4/1/2021):

1. Marco Luciano, SS
2. Joey Bart, C
3. Heliot Ramos, OF
4. Hunter Bishop, OF
5. Patrick Bailey, C
6. Will Wilson, SS
7. Luis Matos, OF
8. Luis Toribio, 3B
9. Alexander Canario, OF
10. Logan Webb, RHP

When I agreed to write all 30 of these 25U lists back in the fall, the first thing I did was put together a spreadsheet of all of the 40-man players who were eligible here who aren't rookie-eligible. The Giants had exactly one entry on my list—Logan Webb—and I wasn't even sure if he was going to make the list. He's a back-of-the-rotation starter or bulk guy type and I decided that was probably better than Seth Corry. So, basically, there's not a lot going on here.

Part 3: Featured Articles

Giants All-Time Top 10 Players

by Rob Mains

POSITION PLAYERS

BUSTER POSEY, C (2009-2019)
The question is whether he can hold on to complete a Hall of Fame-worthy career after opting out of 2020. He was Rookie of the Year in 2010 and MVP two years later when he led the league with a .336 batting average and had career highs in hits, doubles, homers, RBI, on-base percentage, and slugging percentage. But he was still one of the league's top hitters as recently as 2017, when he hit .320/.400/.462. Here's hoping he can pick up from there.

BILL TERRY, 1B (1923-1936)
The last National Leaguer to hit .400 (.401/.452/.619 in 1930, with 254 hits, the most in NL history), Terry's .899 career OPS is the sixth-highest in team history (min. 3000 plate appearances), albeit accumulated in the Lively Ball Era. He didn't have a lot of power, hitting more than 15 homers in a season only four times, but he was a fine fielder who scored 100 runs seven times and drove in 100 six times. He managed the club from 1932 to 1941, winning three pennants and a World Series. His career totals might have been higher but early on he was blocked by George Kelly. He also drove a hard bargain, refusing to play baseball at a discount when he could make more money elsewhere.

WILLIE McCOVEY, 1B (1959-1973, 1977-1980)
He had one of the great rookie seasons ever, hitting .354/.429/.656 in just 52 games in 1959 to win the top honor. Blocked by Orlando Cepeda and other graduates of one of the most fecund farms in history, he didn't get a full-time starting role until 1963; he promptly led the league with 44 homers. His most

devastating peak was 1968-70, when he hit .300/.425/.603, averaging 40 homers and 119 RBI per year and leading the league in OPS every season. He returned to the club in 1977 and at age 39 clubbed 28 homers and slugged .500.

LARRY DOYLE, 2B (1907-1916)
Called "Laughing Larry" for his sunny disposition, Doyle was the Giants' first MVP, winning the award in 1912 on the strength of a .330/.393/.471 batting line with 98 runs, 91 RBI, and 36 stolen bases. His .292/.359/.411 line as a Giant stood out in the Deadball Era; as his OPS was 27 percent better than average. He had pop, leading the league in doubles and triples once each, and stole 291 bases, third in franchise history.

ART FLETCHER, SS (1909-1920)
Fletcher was a scrappy, brawling Deadball Era player, gladly getting in the way of pitches to get on base (he was in the top four in the league in getting hit for ten straight years, leading it five times). He combined decent batting (his .275/.318/.356 line as a Giant was league average), speed (he stole as many as 32 bases in a season), and one of the best shortstop gloves in the game. Doyle's double play partner helped the Giants to four National League pennants with the club.

TRAVIS JACKSON, SS (1922-1936)
Jackson was an outstanding player but he's not well-remembered despite being a Hall of Famer because he never led the league in any offensive category. Often injured, he also had a short peak. A shortstop who hits .291/.337/.433 with a dozen or so homers has value, though, in any era. He struggled defensively early in his career (58 errors in 1924) but greatly improved and had a powerful arm, leading the league in shortstop assists four times. His nickname, "Stonewall," referred to his ability to keep balls from passing him.

MEL OTT, OF (1926-1947)
In 35 games as a 17-year-old in 1926, Ott hit .383/.393/.417 and still had a .910 OPS 19 years later at 36. The compact 5'9" slugger could do it all: .304 career average (all with the Giants), 511 homers, .947 OPS (behind only Mays and Bonds), 1,708 walks and .414 on-base percentage (both second to Bonds). His home run totals were inflated by playing his home games at the Polo Grounds, but he hit for a better average, with far more doubles and triples, on the road. He became manager in 1942, while still a player, and managed for seven seasons, during which the New York press took to calling the team the "Otters." It was Ott to whom Leo Durocher was referring when he supposedly said, "Nice guys finish last," but that was more an indictment of Leo's values than Mel's character.

WILLIE MAYS, OF (1951-1972)

In 1969, baseball celebrated its centenary, and in a vote of sportswriters, Joe DiMaggio was named the greatest living player. In his career, DiMaggio had a .977 OPS, 55 percent above average, with 361 home runs in 1,736 games. To that point in his career, in a much tougher offensive environment, Mays had a .962 OPS, 60 percent above average, with 587 home runs in 2,446 games. Mays was simply the most complete player ever, blasting 646 homers with the Giants, stealing 336 bases, playing a superlative center field, and making probably the most famous defensive play in history.

BOBBY BONDS, OF (1968-1974)

Barry's dad was born too early. Fans and writers focused on his prodigious strikeout totals—he led the league three times, was in the top three every year he was a regular, and set a single-season record that lasted 36 years—instead of his many strengths. In a low-offense era, he had power (186 homers), speed (263 stolen bases and an outstanding 81 percent success rate), and on-base skills (.356 on-base percentage with as many as 95 walks in a season). And he was a strong fielder with a cannon arm, winning three Gold Gloves. He defined the 30-30 season, reaching the dual milestone five times, and yet teams didn't know what to do with him.

BARRY BONDS, OF (1993-2007)

I know, but he hit 586 homers for the Giants, and his 1.143 OPS for the club is almost double the park-adjusted average for those years. In his early years with the club he was an outstanding fielder, winning five Gold Gloves. He was intentionally walked an absurd 575 times with the team; next on the career list is Albert Pujols with 312, and we can't quantify all the times teams pitched around him. Between 2001 and 2004 he reached base in over half his plate appearances. Only five other players have done that even once, and only Babe Ruth did it more often. PEDs might have played a role in his accomplishments, but they weren't responsible for that.

PITCHERS

CHRISTY MATHEWSON, RHP (1900-1916)

Mathewson's accomplishments are otherworldly by today's standards. He led the league in ERA five times, with figures of 1.14, 1,28, 1.43, 1.99, 2.06. His career figure of 2.12 as a Giant is scarcely higher. He pitched more than 300 innings 11 times. He won 22 or more games twelve seasons in a row, with 30 or more four times. He won 372 games as a Giant. He led the league in strikeouts five times and had the highest K/BB ratio nine times. He allowed fewer than a walk per nine innings five times, an unapproachable record, and his 1905 World Series performance—three complete-game shutouts—will never be equaled. And he was a college-educated gentleman superstar, helping baseball shed its ruffian image.

JOE McGINNITY, RHP (1902-1908)

He led the league in games pitched in five of his six full seasons as a Giant and threw 434 innings in 1903 and 408 in 1904, earning the "Iron Man" nickname. He was 31-20 in 1903, starting more than one in three games, and going 6-0 in three August doubleheaders in which he started both ends. He joined the Giants midway through the 1902 season, jumping with his manager, John McGraw, from the American League back when the two leagues fought over players. He and Mathewson formed one of the most storied 1-2 top-of-the-rotation combinations in history.

CARL HUBBELL, LHP (1928-1943)

The Tigers signed him 1925 but player-manager Ty Cobb didn't care for Hubbell's screwball, urging him to discard it, and the Giants bought him from Detroit three years later. "The Meal Ticket" became the ace on the great Giants teams of the 1930s, named to every All-Star team from 1933 to 1938, a streak during which he averaged 21-10 with a 2.58 ERA and led the league in starts, innings, complete games, shutouts, wins, and ERA. In the 1934 All-Star Game he struck out Hall of Famers Babe Ruth, Lou Gehrig, Jimmie Foxx, Al Simmons, and Joe Cronin in a row. After retiring, he became a very successful Giants farm director.

SAL MAGLIE, RHP (1945, 1950-1955)

His nickname was "The Barber" because of his propensity to pitch inside. With the Giants, he hit one of every 175 batters he faced. (In 2020, major league pitchers hit batters more than twice as frequently, one of 81 batters. It's relative.) Maglie spent five years in the minors with three organizations, got a call to the majors in 1945, jumped to the Mexican League in 1946, and was consequently banned from American baseball until 1950. That year, at 33, he played his first full season in the majors. He said that pitching in the arid Mexican air helped him perfect his signature curve, and the results bore him out; he went 18-4 with a league-leading 2.71 ERA. He followed that with 23-6 and 18-8 seasons with sub-3.00 ERAs.

JOHNNY ANTONELLI, LHP (1954-1960)

His best season with the Giants was his first, following a trade from Milwaukee for 1951 hero Bobby Thomson. He went 21-7 in 37 starts, leading the league with a 2.30 ERA and six shutouts. From 1954 to 1959, he led the Giants in starts, innings, strikeouts, wins, ERA, complete games, and shutouts, all by comfortable margins. He disliked playing on the west coast, though, following the Giants' move to San Francisco after the 1957 season, and had pitched himself out of the rotation in 1960, out of San Francisco in 1961, and out of baseball in 1962. Adjusted for season and park, his 3.13 Giants ERA is second to Hubbell by a lefty in team history.

JUAN MARICHAL, RHP (1960-1973)

Marichal had the misfortune to pitch at the apex of Sandy Koufax and Bob Gibson's careers, or he'd likely be known as the best National League pitcher of his era. From 1962 to 1969, he averaged a 22-10 record with a 2.46 ERA, 285 innings, 23 complete games, and 207 strikeouts, striking out 3.9 batters for every one he walked. But he trailed Gibson in strikeouts and Koufax in ERA, winning percentage, OPS allowed, and K/BB, finishing second in each category. As a result, though he was an All-Star every year, he won no Cy Young Awards while Koufax and Gibson combined for five. The first great pitcher from the Dominican Republic is, with Hubbell and Mathewson, one of the franchise's three greatest pitchers.

GAYLORD PERRY, RHP (1962-1971)

He was remarkably durable, averaging 38 starts and 296 innings with an 18-13 record per year from 1966 to 1971, with a 2.75 ERA that was 28 percent better than league average. He was constantly accused of throwing a spitball. A TV reporter asked his five-year-old daughter, Allison, seated in the stands during one of Perry's 1971 NLCS starts, whether her daddy threw a greaseball. "It's a hard slider," she replied. Apparently thinking they were bailing on Perry a year too early rather than a year too late, the Giants dealt him to Cleveland for Sam McDowell in November 1971. As it turned out, they were just a little off—he only had 410 games, 180 wins, and two Cy Young Awards to go.

JIM BARR, RHP (1971-1978, 1982-1983)

The Giants were a struggling franchise in the 1970s, finishing below .500 during Barr's tenure and failing to draw even a million fans to Candlestick Park in all but his first and last seasons. At his peak, from 1972 to 1976, he was the team's best pitcher, averaging 229 innings and a 3.08 ERA, 21 percent below the league average, adjusted for Candlestick. Outstanding control was his calling card; among Giants pitchers with at least 1,000 innings with the club, his 5.2 percent walk rate ranks sixth-lowest.

MATT CAIN, RHP (2005-2017)

Cain turned 28 just before the 2012 postseason, which culminated in the second Giants championship in three years. To that point in his career, he had a 3.27 ERA, 24 percent below average, to go with a .657 OPS allowed over 235 starts. He had a 4-2 record and 2.10 ERA in eight postseason starts. Over the prior four seasons, he'd been named to three All-Star teams and received votes for three

Cy Young Awards. From that point forward, as elbow and hamstring problems became chronic: 96 starts, 4.82 ERA, 22 percent above average, .781 OPS allowed, no awards, no postseasons.

MADISON BUMGARNER, LHP (2009-2019)
His heroics in the 2014 postseason—six starts and a relief appearance, 1.03 ERA, MVP of the Championship Series and World Series—cemented his place in Bay Area lore. They came in the middle of a run from 2011 to 2016 during which he led National League pitchers in starts, innings, wins (93, 39 more than anyone else), ERA (3.00), OPS allowed (.634), and strikeouts (average 214 per season). He made at least 31 starts, pitched at least 200 innings, and was credited with at least 13 wins each year. Only 31, he's still going, but it seems certain that the Giants got the best part of his career.

A Taxonomy of 2020 Abnormalities

by Rob Mains

I'm going to start this with a trivia question. Trust me, it's relevant. Don't bother skipping to the end of the article to find the answer, it's not there.

Only five players have appeared in 140 or more games for 16 straight seasons. Who are they?

It's a trivia question starting off an essay, so you know how this works: Whatever you guessed, you're wrong. It's okay. As someone who purchased this book, chances are good that you're an educated baseball fan. But the circumstances behind 2020 force us to abandon, or at least seriously question, some of our favorite patterns and crutches for evaluating the game we love.

We just completed what was undoubtedly the strangest season in MLB history. No fans, geographically limited schedule, universal DH, seven-inning twin bills, runners on second in extra innings, a 16-team postseason, a club playing at a Triple-A stadium. Some of these changes will likely persist (sorry), but we've never had so many tweaks dumped on us all at once, at least not since they figured out how many balls were in a walk.

And the biggest, of course, was the 60-game season. The 19th century was dotted with teams that went bankrupt before the season ended, but the lone season with only 60 scheduled games was 1877. That year there were only six teams, the league rostered a total of 77 players (just 16 more than the 2020 Marlins), and batters called for pitches to be thrown high or low by the pitcher, who was 50 feet away. We can say the 2020 season was easily the shortest ever for recognizable baseball.

As such, it'll stand out. Few abbreviated seasons do. Just about everybody reading this knows the 1994 season ended after Seattle's Randy Johnson struck out Oakland's Ernie Young for the last out of the Mariners-A's game on August 11. The ensuing player strike wiped out the rest of the season and the postseason. Teams played only 112-117 games that year.

And many of you know that a strike in the middle of the 1981 season split the season in two, resulting in the only Division Series until 1995. Teams played only 103-111 games that year, the shortest regular season since 1885.

San Francisco Giants 2021

Those two seasons are memorable. So when we see that nobody drove in 100 runs in 1981, or that Greg Maddux was the only pitcher with 180 or more innings pitched in 1994, we think, "Of course. Strike year."

But we don't remember other short years. You might not recall that the 1994 strike spilled into the next year, chopping 18 games off the 1995 schedule. You might've read that the 1918 season, played during the last pandemic, ended after Labor Day due to the government's World War I "work or fight" order. A strike erased the first week and a half of the 1972 season, but that year's best known as the last time pitchers batted in the American League.

The point is, while we don't remember small changes to the schedule, we remember the big ones. The 1981 mid-season strike. The 1994 season- and Series-ending strike. And, of course, the pandemic-shortened 2020 season. We won't need a reminder why Marcell Ozuna's 18 homers were the fewest to lead the National League in a century. (Literally; Cy Williams led with 15 in 1920.)

Now, about that trivia question. The five players are Hank Aaron, Brooks Robinson, Pete Rose, Ichiro Suzuki, and Johnny Damon. The one nobody gets, of course, is Damon, and a lot of people miss Ichiro, whose last season of 140-plus games came garbed in the red-orange and ocean blue of Miami when he was 42. That's half of what makes it a good question. The other half is the two guys whom many think made the list but didn't. Lou Gehrig? His streak started in the Yankees' 42nd game of the 1925 season and lasted only 13 seasons after that. And everybody assumes Cal Ripken Jr. did it, having played 2,632 straight games over 17 seasons. But one of those 17 seasons was 1994, when the Orioles played only 112 games.

My point? *I just told you* everybody remembers the 1994 strike year, but everybody forgets it fell in the middle of Ripken's streak, separating the first twelve years from the last four. Just because we recall something doesn't mean it's always at the front of our minds.

Nobody is going to forget 2020, and baseball is obviously not the main reason. But there will come a time in the future when you're looking at a player's or a team's record, and there will be baffling numbers there for 2020, and you'll think, "I wonder what happened." (Not to mention the missing line for minor league players.) Just like you forgot that the 1994 strike limited Ripken to 112 games.

Try not to forget it, though. The 2020 season resulted in weird statistical results for several reasons.

There were only 60 games.
I know, duh. But that had impacts beyond counting stats like Ozuna's home run total or Yu Darvish and Shane Bieber leading the majors with eight wins. (I know, pitcher wins, but still.)

The 162-game season is the longest among major North American sports, and that duration gives us a gift. Over the course of a long season, small variations tend to even out. A player who has a ten-game hot streak will probably have a ten-game cold streak. A team that starts the year losing a bunch of close games will probably win a bunch of them. We get regression to the mean. Statistics stabilize.

Consider flipping a coin. Over the long run, we expect it to come up heads about half the time. But the fewer flips, the more variation there'll be. If you flip a coin six times, probability theory tells us you'll get at least two-third heads about 34 percent of the time. Flip it 30 times, your chance of two-thirds heads drops to five percent.

Or, relevant to this case, if you flip a coin 60 times, your chance of getting at least 36 heads—that's 60 percent—is 7.75 percent. Expand the coin-flipping to 162 times, and the chance of getting 60 percent heads drops to 0.73 percent.

In other words, the odds of an outcome that's 20 percent better (or worse) than expected is *more than ten times higher* when you flip your coin 60 times than when you do it 162 times. Call it small sample size, call lack of mean reversion, or call it luck not evening out, 162 is a lot more predictive than 60. You get much more variation over 60 games than over 162. Bieber's 1.63 ERA and 0.87 FIP aren't something we'd see over a full season, and neither is Javier Baéz's .203/.238/.360.

Some players' lines in 2020 look normal. Brian Anderson had an .811 OPS in 2019 and an .810 OPS in 2020. (He probably would have gotten that last point if he'd been given enough time.) But there are many like Bieber and Baéz, some of them from young players still establishing their talent levels. The answer to the question, "What went right or wrong for that guy in 2020?" is most likely "Nothing, it was just a 2020 thing."

Preseason training was abbreviated for hitters.

Every year, spring training drags. Players get tired of it, fans get tired of it, and you sure can tell sportswriters get tired of it. Yes, something to get everyone into shape is necessary, but does it really have to drag on for over a month? Can't we shorten it?

The 2020 season answered in the negative, at least for hitters. Warren Spahn is credited with saying that hitting is timing and pitching is upsetting timing. It appears nobody had his timing down after the abbreviated July summer camp. Through August 9—18 games into the season—MLB batters were hitting .230/.311/.395 with a .275 BABIP. That BABIP, had it held, would have been the lowest since 1968, the Year of the Pitcher. In recent years it's hovered around .300.

It didn't hold. Play returned to more normal levels the rest of the year: .249/.325/.425 with a .297 BABIP starting August 10. But batters whose play concentrated in those first two weeks wound up with ugly lines. Andrew

Benintendi went on the injured list with a season-ending rib cage strain on August 11. His final line: .103/.314/.128 in 14 games. Franchy Cordero went on the IL with a hamate bone fracture on August 9 and a .154/.185/.231 line. Even though he came back strong in a late September return, it was too late to repair his full-season numbers.

Preseason training was abbreviated for pitchers.

Every year, spring training drags. Players get tired of it, fans get tired of it ... wait, I already said that. But the abbreviated preseason was tough on pitchers, too. As noted, they had the upper hand coming out of the gate. But then they lost that hand. And then their arms, too.

The 2020 season was spread over 67 days. During those 67 days, 237 pitchers hit the Injured List, compared to 135 in the first 67 days of 2019. A lot of those IL stints, though, were COVID-19-related. Still, over the first 67 days of the 2019 season, there were 72 pitchers on the IL with arm injuries. That figure jumped to 110 in 2020, a 53 percent increase.

There are a number of factors contributing to pitcher arm injuries, ranging from usage to velocity, but it appears that attenuated preseason training played a role. A lot of pitchers had super-short seasons due to arm woes. Corey Kluber, Roberto Osuna, and Shohei Ohtani combined for seven innings, none after August 8. All suffered arm injuries. We'll never know whether they'd have fared better with a longer preseason, but we can guess how they probably feel.

Everybody played.

Rosters were set to expand from 25 to 26 in 2020, so even if we'd had a normal season, we'd have likely seen 2019's record of 1,410 players on MLB rosters broken. But due to the pandemic, rosters started the year at 30 and were cut to only 28. Add multiple COVID-19 absences and the revolving door caused by poor starts by hitters and a rash of pitcher arm injuries, and 1,289 players appeared in MLB games in 2020. The comparable figure over the first 67 days of the 2019 season was 1,109. That 16 percent increase works out to an average of six more players per team in 2020 compared to a similar slice of 2019. A future look back at 2020 rosters will include a lot of unfamiliar names.

Plus became a minus.

In advanced metrics, we adjust batter and pitcher performance for park and league/era variations. A plus sign appended to the end of a measure means that it's adjusted for park and league. It's scaled to an average of 100, with higher figures above average and lower figures below average. (Similarly, a metric with a minus is also park- and league-adjusted and scaled to 100, with lower values better.) Here at BP, our advanced measure of offensive performance is DRC+. Baseball-Reference has OPS+ and FanGraphs has wRC+.

Using park and league adjustments, we can compare Dante Bichette's 1995 Steroid Era season at pre-humidor Coors Field (.340/.364/.620, 40 homers, 128 RBI, MVP runner-up) with Jim Wynn's 1968 Year of the Pitcher season at the cavernous Astrodome (.269/.376/.474, 26 homers, 67 RBI, no MVP votes). It's not close. DRC+, OPS+, and wRC+ all give the nod to Wynn, handily. This is a useful tool. As my Baseball Prospectus colleague Patrick Dubuque tweeted last fall, "Please note that when I ask how you are, I am already adjusting for era."

The 2020 season messes up plus (and minus) stats for two reasons. First, the park adjustment was based on only 30 home games instead of the usual 81. Everything noted above regarding the short season applies, literally doubly, to park effect calculations. DRC+ uses a single-season park factor. OPS+ uses a three-year average and wRC+ five years. The figure for 2020 is suspect.

Second, OPS+ and wRC+ adjust for league: American and National. (DRC+ adjusts for opponent, regardless of league.) While there were two leagues in 2020, they were an artificial construct. To reduce travel, teams played opponents geographically, not based on league. There weren't two leagues, American and National. There were three, Western, Central, and Eastern.

That makes a difference because teams in the same league played in different run-scoring environments. AL teams scored 4.58 runs per game, NL teams 4.71. That's a small difference. But teams in the East scored 0.21 more runs per game (4.95) than teams in the West (4.74), and they both scored a lot more than Central teams (4.25). Adjusting for league misses that difference, so this book will be safe in that regard, but other sources may be distorted somewhat.

Not every game was a "game."
In 2020, the rising tide of strikeouts was finally stemmed. Strikeouts per team per game fell from 8.8 in 2019 to 8.7 in 2020. That marked the first decline after 14 straight annual increases.

In 2020, the rising tide of strikeouts rose higher. Batters struck out in 23.4 percent of plate appearances compared to 23.0 percent in 2019. That marked the 15th straight annual increase.

Both are true statements.

Because of two rule changes—seven-inning doubleheaders and runners on second in extra innings—games in 2020 were unprecedented in their brevity. There were 37.0 plate appearances per game in 2020. The only years with fewer were 1904 and 1906-1909. The average game in 2020 entailed 8.61 innings pitched, the fewest since 1899.

So when you see any per-game stats for 2020, you need to increase them by 3 or 4 percent to get them on equal footing with recent years.

San Francisco Giants 2021

   Or, better, just ignore them. Last year happened. There were major league games contested between major league teams. But when you're looking at those physical or electronic baseball cards, when you're weaving narratives over why this young player's inevitable rise to stardom fell apart or why that old veteran rekindled his magic, don't linger on the 2020 line. It was just too weird.

Thanks to Lucas Apostoleris for research assistance.

—Rob Mains is an author of Baseball Prospectus.

Tranches of WAR

by Russell A. Carleton

We ask "replacement level" to be a lot of things. Sometimes contradictory things. Sometimes I wonder if we know what it even means anymore. The original idea was that it represented the level of production that a team could expect to get from "freely available talent", including bench players, minor leaguers, and waiver wire pickups. It created a common benchmark to compare everyone to, and for that reason, it represented an advancement well beyond what was available at the time. In fact, it created a language and a framework for evaluating players that was not just better but *entirely* different than what came before it.

But then we started mumbling in that language. The idea behind "wins above replacement" was one part sci-fi episode and one part mathematical exercise. Imagine that a player had disappeared before the season and suddenly, in an alternate timeline, his team would have had to replace him. The distance between him and that replacement line was his value. We need to talk about that alternate timeline.

Without getting too into 2:00 am "deep conversations" with extensive navel-gazing, it's worth thinking about why one player might not be playing, while another might.

- A player might not be playing because he has a short-term injury or his manager believes that he needs a day off.
- A player might not be playing because he has a longer-term injury that requires him to be on the injured list.

There's a difference here between these two situations. In particular, the first one generally *doesn't* involve a compensatory roster move, while the second one does. It's possible, though not guaranteed, that the person who will be replacing the injured/resting player would be the same in either case. That matters. Teams generally carry a spare part for all eight position players on the diamond, although in the era of a four-player bench, those spare parts usually are the backup plan for more than one spot.

San Francisco Giants 2021

A couple of years ago, I posed a hypothetical question. Suppose that a team had two players in its system fighting for a fourth outfielder spot. One of them was a league average hitter, but would be worth 20 runs below average if allowed to play center field for a full season. One of them was a perfectly average fielder, but would be 15 runs below average as a hitter, if allowed to play an entire season. Which of the two should the team roster? It's tempting to say the second one, as overall, he is the better player. That misses the point. A league average hitter on the bench isn't just a potential replacement for an injured outfielder. He might also pinch hit for the light-hitting shortstop in a key spot. You keep the average hitter on the roster, even though he isn't a hand-in-glove fit for one specific place on the field, because being a bench player is a different job description than being a long-term fill-in for someone. If you find yourself in need of a longer-term fill-in, you can bring the other guy up from AAA.

When we're determining the value of an everyday player though, if he had disappeared before the season and a team would have had to replace his production, they likely would have done it with a player who was a long-term fill-in type because they would have had to replace a guy who played everyday. Maybe that's the same guy that they would have rostered on their bench anyway, but we don't know. It gets to the query of what we hope to accomplish with WAR. Are we looking for an accurate modeling of reality or are we looking for a common baseline to compare everyone to? Both have their uses, but they are somewhat different questions.

Let's talk about another dichotomy.

- A player might not be playing because he isn't very good and is a bench-level player.
- A player might not be playing because there is another player on the team who has a situational advantage that makes him the better choice today. The classic case of this is a handedness platoon. On another day, he might be a better choice.

When we think about player usage, I think we're still stuck in the model that there are starters and there are scrubs. We have plenty of words for bench players or reserves or backups or utility guys. We do still have the word "platoon" in our collective vocabulary, but in the age of short benches, it's hard to construct one. It's always been hard to construct them. You have to find two players who hit with different hands, have skill sets that complement each other, and probably play the same position. In the era of the short bench, one of them had probably better double as a utility player in some way. Baseball has a two-tiered language geared toward the idea of regulars and reserves. The fact that it was so easy for me to find plenty of synonyms for "a player whose primary function is to come into a game to replace a regular player if he is injured or resting" should tell you something.

I'm always one to look for "unspoken words" in baseball. What is it called when someone is both half of a platoon and the utility infielder? That guy exists sometimes, but he reveals himself in that role—usually by accident. We don't have a word for that, and whenever I find myself saying "we don't have a word for that", I look for new opportunities. What do you call it, further, when the job of being the utility infielder is decentralized across the whole infield with occasional contributions from the left fielder? It's not even a "super-utility" player. What happens when you build your entire roster around the idea that everyone will be expected to be a triple major?

⚾ ⚾ ⚾

I think someone else beat me to this one, and on a grand scale. Platoons work because we know that hitters of the opposite hand to the pitcher get better results than hitters of the same hand, usually to the tune of about 20 points of OBP. If you want to express that in runs, it usually comes out to somewhere around 10 to 12 runs of linear weights value prorated across 650 PA. But hang on a second, now let's say that we have two players who might start today, both of roughly equal merit with the bat. One has a handedness advantage, but is the worse fielder of the two. In that case, as long as his "over the course of a season" projection as a fielder at whatever position you want to slot him into is less than a 10-run drop from the guy he might replace, then he's a better option today.

We're not used to thinking of utility players as bat-first options, who would play below-average defense at three different infield positions. That guy might hook on as a 2B/3B/LF type (Howie Kendrick, come on down!) but teams usually think to themselves that they need as their utility infielder someone who "can handle" shortstop, the toughest of the infield spots to play. If someone can do that *and* hit well, he's probably already starting somewhere, so he's not available as a utility infielder. It's easier for those glove guys to find a job. In a world where the replacement for a shortstop *has to be* the designated utility infielder, that makes sense.

But as we talked about last week, we're living in a different world. The rate at which a replacement for a regular starter turns out to be *another starter* shifting over to cover has gone way up over the last five years. There was always some of it in the game, but this has been a supernova of switcheroos. Now if your second baseman is capable of playing a decent shortstop, that 2B/3B/LF guy can swap in. He's not actually playing shortstop, and maybe the defense suffers from the switch, but if he's got enough of a bat, he might outhit those extra fielding miscues. And in doing so, he is effectively your backup shortstop.

Somewhere along the lines, teams got hip to the idea of multi-positional play from their regulars. I've written before about how you can't just put a player, however athletic, into a new position and expect much at first. The data tell us that. Eventually, players can learn to be multi-positionalists, but it takes time, roughly on the order of two months, before they're OK. But there's a hidden message in there. If you give a player some reps at a new spot, he's a reasonably gifted athlete and somewhat smart and willing to learn, he could probably pick it up enough to get to "good enough," and it doesn't take forever. You just have to be purposeful about it. Maybe you get to the point where you can start to say "he's still below average but we could move him there and get another bat into the lineup, and it's a net win."

Teams have started to build those extra lessons into their player development program. It used to be seen as a mark of weakness to be relegated to "utility player" because that meant that you were a bench player (all those synonyms above come with a side of stigma). Now, it's a way of building a team. If you get a few reps in the minors (where it doesn't count) at a spot, you'll have at least played the spot at game speed before. There are limits to how far you can push that. A slow-footed "he's out in left field because we don't have the DH" guy is never going to play short, but maybe your third baseman can try second base and not look like a total moose out there.

⚾ ⚾ ⚾

Back to WAR. I'd argue that the world of starters and scrubs is slowly disintegrating, for good cause. In the event that a regular starter really does go down with an injury–ostensibly, the alternate universe scenario that WAR is attempting to model–it makes the team a little more resilient to replacing him. And the good news is that you're more likely to be able to replace him with the best of the bench bunch, rather than the third-best guy, because the best guy doesn't have to be an exact positional match for the guy who got hurt. And that's what the manager would want to do. He'd want to replace that long-term production, not with an amalgam of everyone else who played that position, but with the best guy available from his reserves.

Now this is still WAR. We still want to retain the principle that we should be measuring a player, and not his teammates. We need some sort of common baseline, and despite what I just said, we'll still need some sort of amalgam. To construct that, I give to you the idea of the tranche. The word, if you've not heard it before, refers to a piece of a whole that is somehow segmented off. It's often used in finance to talk about layers of a financial instrument.

Here, I want you to consider that there are 30 starters at each of the seven non-battery positions (catchers should have their own WAR, since only a catcher can replace a catcher). We can identify them by playing time, and we can futz around with the definition a little bit if we need to. Next, among those who aren't in that starting pool, we identify the top tranche of the 30 best bench players, which I would again identify by playing time, and then the second and third and fourth and so on. If a player were to disappear, his manager would probably want to take a guy from that top tranche of the bench to replace him. In a world where even the starters can slide around the field, that becomes more feasible.

We can take a look at that top tranche and say "How many of them showed that they are able to play (first, second, etc.)?" and therefore could have directly substituted for the starter? How many of them could have been a direct substitute for our injured player? We don't know whether one of them would be on *a specific* team, but we can say that 40 percent of the time, a manager would have been able to draw from tranche 1 in filling the role, and 35 percent from tranche 2. But on tranche 1, we can also look at how many of those players played a position that could have then shifted and covered for that spot. We'd need some eligibility criteria for all of this (probably a minimum number of games played) but it would just be a matter of multiplication. Shortstop would be harder to fill, and managers would probably be dipping a little further down in the talent pool, and so replacement level would be lower, as it is now.

Doing some quick analysis, I found that the difference in just batting linear weights (haven't even gotten into running or fielding) between tranche 1 and tranche 2 in 2019 was about 6.5 runs, prorated across 650 PA. Between tranche 1 and tranche 3, it's 10.8 runs. The ability to shift those plate appearances up the ladder has some real value.

This part is important. We can also give credit to starters for the positions that they showed an ability to play, even if they didn't play them (this is the guy fully capable of playing center, but who's in a corner because the team already has a good center fielder) because he allows a team to carry a player who hits like a left fielder to functionally be the team's backup center fielder. He facilitates that movement upward among the tranches. We can start to appreciate the difference between a left fielder who would never be able to hack it in center (and the compensatory move that his team would have to make) and the left fielder who could do it, but just didn't have to very often.

Past that, you can continue to use whatever hitting and fielding and running metrics you like to determine a player's value, but when we get down to constructing that baseline, I'd argue we need a better conceptual and mathematical framework. It's going to require some more #GoryMath than we're used to, but I'd argue it's a better conceptualization of the way that MLB actually plays the game in 2020. If…y'know…MLB plays in 2020. If WAR is going to be our flagship statistic among the *acronymati*, then we need to acknowledge that it contains some old and starting-to-be-out-of-date assumptions about the game. We may need to tinker with it. Here's my idea for how.

—*Russell A. Carleton is an author of Baseball Prospectus.*

Secondhand Sport

by Patrick Dubuque

Back before time stopped, I liked to go to thrift stores. Now that I'm older, I rarely ever buy anything—I don't need much in my life, now—but I still enjoy the old familiar circuit: check to see if there are baseball cards to write about, look for board or card games to play with the kids, scan for random ironic jerseys, hit the book section. It takes ten, maybe fifteen minutes. Thrift stores are the antithesis of modern online shopping, because you don't know what they have, and you don't even really know what you want. It's junk, literal junk, stuff other people thought was worthless. That's what makes it great.

In an idealized economy, thrift stores shouldn't exist. Everybody has a living wage, and every product has a durability that exactly matches its desired life; nothing should need to be given away, no one should need to be given to. But then, thrift stores shouldn't work on a customer experience level, either. You wouldn't think an ethos of "let's make everything disorganized and hard to find" would lead to customer satisfaction, but low-budget retailers like TJ Maxx and Ross thrive on this model. People like bargain hunting as much for the hunting as the bargain; it's part of the experience, spending time as if it's a wager. There's a thrill, occasionally, in inefficiency.

In sports, the modern overuse of the word "inefficiency" is a condemnation: It insinuates that there is *an* efficiency, a correct way to be found, and that all other ways are wrong ways. It's prevalent in baseball but hardly contained to it; the lifehack, the Silicon Valley disruption are other examples of productivity creep in our daily lives. Their modern success makes plenty of sense. Maximization of resources, after all, is its own puzzle, and an industry of European board games is founded upon it. It's fun to take a system and optimize it, unravel it like a sudoku puzzle. If there's only one kind of genius, after all, there's no way anyone can fail to appreciate it.

Baseball has been hacking away at these perceived inefficiencies since its inception: platoons, bullpens, farm systems were all installed to extract more out of the tools at hand. But it's been a particular badge of the sabermetric movement, from Ken Phelps and his All-Star Team to Ricardo Rincon and the darlings of *Moneyball*. It's business, but it's also an ethos: the idea that there's treasure among the trash, something we all failed to appreciate until someone brought it to light.

It's the myth that made Sidd Finch so enticing, that fuels so many "best shape" narratives and new pitch promises. We all, athletes and unathletic sportswriters, want to believe that there's genius trapped inside us, and that it's just a matter of puzzling out the combination to unlock it. That our art, our style is the next inefficiency, waiting for our own Billy Beane. It's why we root for underdogs, and why we're excited for the Mike Tauchmans and the Eurubiel Durazos, champions of skin-deep mediocrity.

Except we aren't anymore, really. The days of "Free X" have descended beyond the ring of irony and into obscurity. There are still Xs to be freed, or at least one X, duplicated endlessly: Mike Ford, Luke Voit, Max Muncy. The undervalued one-dimensional slugger demonstrated how the game hasn't quite culturally caught up to its logical extreme. But for those who don't fit the rather spacious mold, times are grimmer. As Rob Arthur revealed several months ago, there's been a marked increase in the number of sub-replacement relievers. It's the outcome of a greater number of teams forced to play out games without the talent to win them, but it's also emblematic of the modern tendency of teams to dispose of their disposable assets, burning through cost-controlled arms the way that man chopped down forests in *The Lorax*. Stuff just isn't built to outlive their original owners anymore.

It's unsurprising, given how well-mined the market for inefficiencies has been of late. The disciples of the early analytics departments, and the disciples of those, have proliferated the league, with only a few backwater holdouts. The league has grown smarter, but every team has learned the same lesson. In fact, the phenomenon creates a peculiar kind of feedback loop: As teams value a specific subset of players or skills, prospective athletes learn to increase their own marketability by conforming themselves to the demands of their prospective employers.

And that's tragic, in the way that the extinction of animals is tragic; a certain amount of biodiversity in baseball has been lost. Shortstops hit like outfielders. Pitchers don't hit at all. Only the catchers remain idiosyncratic, thanks to the defensive demands of their position; eventually they too will be required to produce like everyone else, or they'll meet the fate of their battery mates. A perfect economy requires perfect production.

I mentioned earlier that more and more, I leave thrift stores empty-handed. It is true that I am more discerning than in the past; my bookshelves are full, and there are more streaming films than I will ever be able to watch. But there are other factors at play.

Thrift stores are, in a way, the bond markets of retail. When the economy is rough and other retailers are struggling, more people look secondhand for their products. But as recently as last year, publications were noting a reversal of the trend: Companies like Goodwill and Savers were expanding despite a strong economy. Publications credited a heightened sense of environmentalism and a rejection of cutting-edge fashion as drivers behind the increase, though the more likely answer is the modern American economy hasn't showered its favors equally, particularly among the young.

But it is more than just the economy. Baseball and thrift stores share something else in common, evident in our current conversations about re-starting the sport: They live in the gray area between public service and private enterprise. Thrift stores provide affordable necessities to lower-class citizens, and collectibles and fashion for the middle-class. Because of the success of the latter, prices have gone up across the board. Especially in terms of clothing, the middle-class flight from fashion into vintage has instead carried the aftereffects of fashion, including its costs, into a territory where people just want clothes. But there's another factor in the rise of prices, in the form of the internet.

The Goodwills of the world have grown smarter, too, employing the internet to extract full value from their detritus. Ebay, similarly, has lost much of the charm it had as a new frontier around the turn of the century. Everything has a price point now; even individual taste is no match for the algorithm, because anything rare, no matter how niche its market, is a collectible to someone.

The internet has had the same effect on thrift stores that sabermetrics has had on baseball; its equivalent to OBP was the bar scanner. As detailed in Slate, the rise of second-party stores on eBay and Amazon birthed an entire industry of used-good salespeople, armed with PDAs and scanners, buying books for three dollars to sell online for five. The author, Michael Savitz, reports earning $60,000 by working nearly 80 hours a week; he makes it clear that this is not a vocation of his choosing. It's long hours, with no real creativity or individuality, skimming the cream off of a local establishment and flipping it to someone with a little more money on the other side of the country. And once the vocation exists, the obvious question arises: why wait to put the wares out on the shelves? Why allow value to exist at all?

Nothing is ruined. Thrift stores will continue to sell polo shirts and DVDs, and baseball will continue to exist and make or lose money, depending on who you believe. But as we continue to refine our knowledge, we lose something in the conquest for efficiency, a delight born out of the unknown. The problem isn't the efficiency itself; we can't blame the booksellers, or the people sweeping freeways to collect grams of platinum from damaged catalytic converters. The problem is a system that requires this sort of profit-skimming behavior in order to feed families (or, for corporations, maximize shareholder return).

In times like these, with the 2020 season on the brink and the collective bargaining agreement close behind, it can often feel like the current situation is untenable. It can't keep going like this, even if we don't know what to do about it. But as with thrift stores, there's an equally irresistible feeling that it *has* to keep going, that it would be unimaginable to not have this broken, amazing sport. Both industries exist on an invisible foundation of friction, of chaos and unpredictability, even as both see their foundations buffed down to a perfect, untouchable polish. But if COVID-19 and its financial ramifications do, as some have suggested, make it such that the baseball that returns is fundamentally different than the baseball that came before, perhaps this is the time to lean in, and change the game even more. Fix bunting. Make defense more difficult. Create viable, alternate strategies. Add some chaos back into baseball. It's fun when no one knows quite where things are.

—*Patrick Dubuque is an author of Baseball Prospectus.*

Steve Dalkowski Dreaming

by Steven Goldman

We dream of being a pitcher, of starring in the major leagues. Depending on your age and your sense of historical perspective, you might imagine yourself as Walter Johnson, throwing harder than anyone else—hitting more batters than anyone else, too, but always feeling bad about it. You could picture yourself as a Tom Seaver or a David Cone, with all the stuff in the world but still being cerebral about it, thinking about so much more than burning 'em in there. There are so many models one could choose: You could be a Lefty Gomez, Jim Bouton, or Bill Lee, skilled, but not taking the whole thing too seriously, or a Lefty Grove, Bob Gibson, or Steve Carlton, powerful but treating each start like a mission to be survived instead of a game to be enjoyed.

Very few would dream of being Steve Dalkowski, the former Baltimore Orioles prospect who died of COVID-19 last week at the age of 80. Yet, there is something just as noble in Dalkowski's negative accomplishments—and accomplishments is what they are—as there is in the precision-engineered pitching of a Greg Maddux. You have to be very good to be that bad. Dalkowski had all of the stuff of the greatest pitchers but none of the command; his story is not one of failing to conquer his limitations, but striving against one of the cruelest hands that fate or genetics or personality can deal us: A desire to achieve great things which is almost but not quite matched by the ability to meet that goal.

As with Johnson, Grove, Bob Feller, and the rest of the hard-throwing pitchers who played before the advent of modern radar guns, we have to take the word of the players and coaches who saw Dalkowski pitch as to his velocity. He was a hard-drinking, maximum-effort pitcher who, if their memories are to be believed, consistently threw over 100 miles per hour. His was the Maltese Fastball, the stuff that dreams are made of. The problem is that velocity without command and control is still a good distance from utility. Dalkowski was the most effective towel you could design for a fish, the sleekest bathing suit intended to be worn by an astronaut, but that doesn't mean he wasn't beautiful: We can appreciate a journey even if it doesn't end at the intended destination.

Whether because of sloppy mechanics he couldn't calm, an inability to understand that a consistent 98 in the strike zone would likely be more effective than a consistent 110 out of it, or all that beer, Dalkowski could never make the adjustments that pitchers like Feller and Nolan Ryan made before him, possibly because he had so far to go: Feller, who never pitched in the minors, came up at 17 and spent three years walking almost seven batters per nine innings before settling in at 3.8 beginning when he was 20. Ryan started out walking over six batters per nine but gradually improved as his long career played out; for him to go from 6.2 walks per nine with the 1966 Greenville Mets to 3.7 with the 1989 Texas Rangers represents a 40 percent reduction. An equivalent improvement by Dalkowski would still have left him walking over 11 batters per nine innings.

Dalkowski was like *The Room* of pitchers, a player so bad he became good again. Cal Ripken, Sr., who both played with and managed Dalkowski, recalled in a 1979 *Sporting News* "where are they now" piece the occasion when the pitcher crossed up his catcher and his fastball, "hit the plate umpire smack in the mask. The mask broke all to pieces and the umpire wound up in the hospital for three days with a concussion. If they ever had a radar gun in those days, I'll bet Dalkowski would have been timed at 110 miles an hour."

Signed by the Orioles out of New Britain High in Connecticut in 1957, Dalkowski was sent to Kingsport in the Appalachian League, where he pitched 62 innings. He allowed only 22 hits in 62 innings, or 3.2 per nine, a number with no equivalent in major league history (though Aroldis Chapman came close in 2014), and also struck out 121 (17.6 per nine) and walked 129 (18.7). He was also charged with 39 wild pitches. That June, one of his fastballs clipped a Dodgers prospect named Bob Beavers and carried away part of his ear. "The first pitch was over the backstop, the second pitch was called a strike, I didn't think it was," Beavers said last year. "The third pitch hit me and knocked me out, so I don't remember much after that. I couldn't get in the sun for a while, and I never did play baseball again." Former minor leaguer Ron Shelton based the *Bull Durham* pitcher Nuke LaLoosh on Dalkowski. And yet, to see him as a figure of fun, an amusing loser, is to misunderstand something unique and strange.

Dalkowski kept on posting some of the strangest lines in baseball history. Pitching for the Stockton Ports of the Class C California League in 1960, he struck out 262 and walked 262 in 170 innings. Yet, he did improve, especially after pitching for Earl Weaver at Elmira in 1962. Weaver had previously had Dalkowski at Aberdeen in 1959, but wasn't ready to grapple with him then. This time he was. "I had grown more and more concerned about players with great physical abilities who could not learn to correct certain basic deficiencies no matter how much you instructed or drilled them," he related in his autobiography, *It's What You Learn After You Know It All That Counts*. He got permission from the Orioles to give all of his players the Stanford-Binet IQ test. "Dalkowski finished in the 1 percentile in his ability to understand facts. Steve, it was said to say, had the ability to do everything but learn." [sic]

IQ tests are problematic diagnostic tools, so take Weaver's estimate of Dalkowski's mental capabilities with a grain of salt. What's important is that even if he got to the right answer by way of the wrong reason, Weaver had learned something valuable. His insight was to stop asking Dalkowski to learn new pitches and just let him get by with the two that he had. Were Dalkowski a prospect today, that would have been a no-brainer: Can't develop a third pitch? The bullpen is right over there, sir. Player development wasn't like that then, but Weaver, temporarily Dalkowski's mentor, could let him work with what he had. According to Weaver, the pitcher responded: "In the final 57 innings he pitched that season Dalkowski gave up 1 earned run, struck out 110 batters, and walked only 11." It's not true—as per the *Elmira Star-Gazette*, as of late July, Dalkowski had walked 71 in 106 innings and finished with 114 in 160 innings, which means Dalkowski's control actually faded at the end of the season rather than improved—but that doesn't mean it didn't happen in some sense, just that it didn't happen that way. Again, it's the journey, not the destination, and his ERA was 3.04 so *something* had gone right.

Also along the way: The next spring, Orioles manager Billy Hitchcock was rooting for Dalkowski to make the team as a long-man—maybe Weaver had gotten through to him. There were things out of Weaver's control, like the universe's twisted sense of humor: that March, Dalkowski's elbow went "twang."

You sometimes read that it was the Orioles' insistence on Dalkowski learning the curve that did him in, but even if they hadn't learned their lesson, the injury was probably just a coincidence: Dalkowski had thrown an incredible number of pitches over the previous few years. Still, it testifies to the dangers of trying to get what you want and risking the loss of what you had. Dalkowski tried to come back, but the 110-mph stuff was gone. A pitcher with no control and no stuff is…a civilian. What followed were years of vagabond living, arrests for drunkenness. There were Alcoholics Anonymous meetings, assistance from baseball alumni associations, but none of it took. From the 1990s until the time of his passing he dwelt in an assisted living facility, suffering from alcohol-related dementia. He'd been a heavy drinker since his teenage years. As with all those pitches per game, there was a price to be paid. You make choices on the journey and some of them are irrevocable. It's like a fairy tale: "Bite of poison apple? Don't mind if I do."

In the aforementioned *Sporting News* profile, Chuck Stevens, the head of the Association of Professional Ballplayers of America, a ballplayer charity, said, "I've got nothing against drinking. I do it myself sometimes. But, I don't condone common drunkenness. We went through lots of heartache and many dollars, but Dalkowski didn't want to help himself and we weren't going to keep him drunk." The journey is *un*like a fairy tale: No one will come along and kiss it better, not if they're busy forming judgments.

In the end, we are left with a sort of philosophical chicken/egg conundrum: Is failing to meet your goals evidence of unfulfilled potential or the lack of it? Isn't what you did by definition what you were capable of doing? Or could you have broken through to something better with the right help, the right lucky break? These are unanswerable questions, and how we try to answer them may say more about us than about the people we're judging.

No pitcher ever has it easy. *All* pitchers must work hard. *All* pitchers must refine their craft. It's almost never just about *stuff*. Dalkowski dreaming is no insult to the great pitchers who made it; from Pete Alexander to Max Scherzer, they have all earned their way up. And yet, if it is true that we can only do as much as we can do, then the journey would be more of an adventure, the ultimate triumph or defeat more noble, if like Dalkowski we lacked 100 percent of the confidence, the command, the self-possession, the commitment, the resistance to making bad decisions that so many great players possess—to be gloriously human. Or, to put it more succinctly, it would be fun to be able to throw as hard as any person ever has. Even if just for a moment, and even if nothing more came of it than that, no one could say you hadn't lived life to the fullest.

—*Steven Goldman is an author of Baseball Prospectus.*

A Reward For A Functioning Society

by Cory Frontin and Craig Goldstein

On July 5, Nationals reliever Sean Doolittle said in the middle of a press conference regarding the restart of Major League Baseball and what would later be known as summer camp, "sports are like the reward of a functioning society." This sentence was amidst a much longer, thoughtful reply about the societal and health conditions under which MLB players were being brought back. It's a very similar sentiment to one Jane McManus used on April 7, when she discussed the White House's meeting with sports commissioners. She said "sports are the effect of a functioning society—not the precursor."

Both versions of the same sentiment spoke to a laudable ideal in the context of a country that was not addressing a rampaging virus, and opting instead to bring sports back for the feeling of normalcy rather than the reality of it. "Priorities," as McManus said.

On Wednesday, the NBA's Milwaukee Bucks conducted a wildcat/political strike, refusing to come out for Game 5 of their playoff series against the Orlando Magic. The Magic refused to accept the forfeit, and shortly thereafter other playoff series were threatened by player strikes. Eventually the league moved to postpone that day's games, folding to players leveraging their united power.

The backdrop against which these actions took place was the shooting by police of Jacob Blake. Blake was shot in the back seven times by police, as he attempted to get into his vehicle. He managed to survive the assault, but is paralyzed from the waist down.

⚾ ⚾ ⚾

The step taken to walk out, first by the Milwaukee Bucks, then subsequently by other NBA, WNBA, and MLB teams, was a step toward upholding the virtue of the sentiment described by McManus and Doolittle. But that sentiment does not align with the broad history of sports in this and other countries, a history that contradicts the core of the idealistic statement.

Sports have been a significant part of American society for most of its existence, expanding in importance and influence in recent years. The idea that society was functioning in a way that was worthy of the reward of sports for most of that time is laughable. Much of America is not functioning and has not functioned for Black people, full stop. The oppressed people at the center of this political act by players, specifically Black players, in concert throughout the NBA and in fits and starts throughout Major League Baseball, have not known a society that functions for them rather than *because* of them.

Politics has been part of the sports landscape since the inception of sport, but for just about as long people have bemoaned its presence. Sports are to be an escape, it is said. An escape from what, though? A functioning society?

No, the presence of sports has never signified a cultural or political system that is on the up and up. Rather, the presence of sports *reflect and reinforce the society that produces them.*

⚾ ⚾ ⚾

The Negro Leagues were born out of societal dysfunction. The need for entirely separate leagues, composed of Black and Latino players barred from the Major Leagues because of racism? That is not a functioning society, and yet there were sports.

Even the integration of players from the Negro Leagues resulted in a transfer of power and wealth from Black-owned businesses and communities and into white ones, mirroring the dysfunction that had bled into every aspect of American society at the time. Japheth Knopp noted in the Spring 2016 Baseball Research Journal:

> *The manner in which integration in baseball—and in American businesses generally—occurred was not the only model which was possible. It was likely not even the best approach available, but rather served the needs of those in already privileged positions who were able to control not only the manner in which desegregation occurred, but the public perception of it as well in order to exploit the situation for financial gain. Indeed, the very word integration may not be the most applicable in this context because what actually transpired was not so much the fair and equitable combination of two subcultures into one equal and more homogenous group, but rather the reluctant allowance—under certain preconditions—for African Americans to be assimilated into white society.*

To understand the value of a movement, though, is not to understand how it is co-opted by ownership, but to know the people it brings together and what they demand. When Jackie Robinson—the player who demarcated the inevitability of the end of the Negro leagues—attended the March on Washington for Jobs and Freedom in 1963, he did so with his family and marched alongside the people. He stood alongside hundreds of thousands to fight for their common civil and labor rights. "The moral arc of the universe is long," many freedom fighters have echoed, "but it bends towards justice." The bend, it is less frequently said, happens when a great mass of people place the moral arc of the universe on their knee and apply force, as Jackie, his family, and thousands of others did that day.

⚾ ⚾ ⚾

Of course, taking the moral arc of the universe down from the mantle and bending it is not without risk. Perhaps the outsized influence of athletes is itself a mark of a dysfunctional society, but, nonetheless, hundreds of athletes woke up on Wednesday morning with the power to bring in millions of dollars in revenues. That very power, as we would come to find out, was matched with the equal and opposite power to *not* bring those revenues. That power, in hands ranging from the Milwaukee Bucks, to Kenny Smith in the *Inside the NBA* Studio, from the unexpected ally, Josh Hader, and his largely white teammates to the notably Black Seattle Mariners, would be exercised for a single demand: the end to state violence against Black people. Not unlike the March itself, it sat at the intersection of the civil rights of Black Americans and bold labor action. The March on Washington stood in the face of a false notion of integration—against an integration of extraction but not one of equality—and proposed something different. Just the same, the acts of solidarity of August 26, 2020 will be remembered in stark defiance of MLB's BLM-branded, but ultimately empty displays on opening weekend.

Bold defiance like this can never be without risk. By choosing to exercise this power, the Milwaukee Bucks took a risk. They risked vitriol and backlash from those they disagreed with. They risked fines or seeing their contracts voided, as a walkout like this is prohibited by their CBA. They risked forfeiting a playoff game, one that, as the No. 1 seed in the playoffs, they'd worked all year to attain. They didn't know how Orlando would respond. It wasn't clear that other teams throughout the league would follow suit in solidarity. And it wasn't known the league would accept these actions and moderately co-opt them by "postponing" games that would have featured no players.

If the league reschedules the games, some of the athletes' risk—their shared sacrifice—will be diminished, in retrospect. But they did not know any of that when they took that risk. And it is often left to athletes to take these risks when others in society won't, especially those of their same socioeconomic status and levels of influence.

It is athletes, specifically BIPOC athletes, that take them, though, because they live with the risk of being something other than white in this country every day. They are no strangers to the realities of police brutality. It seems incongruous then, to say that sports are a reward for a functioning society when we rely on athletes to lead us closer to being a functioning society. Luckily, our beloved athletes, WNBA players first and foremost among them, understand what sports truly are: a pipebender for the moral arc of the universe.

—Craig Goldstein is editor in chief of Baseball Prospectus. Cory Frontin is an author of Baseball Prospectus.

Index of Names

Adon, Melvin 92
Anderson, Tyler 40
Bailey, Patrick 78, 102
Baragar, Caleb 42
Bart, Joey 14, 100
Beede, Tyler 92
Belt, Brandon 79
Bishop, Hunter 80, 101
Brebbia, John 93
Cahill, Trevor 44
Canario, Alexander 80, 104
Casali, Curt 16
Corry, Seth 94, 105
Cozart, Zack 81
Crawford, Brandon 18
Cueto, Johnny 46
Davis, Jaylin 82
DeSclafani, Anthony 48
Dickerson, Alex 83
Dubón, Mauricio 20
Duggar, Steven 84
Flores, Wilmer 22
García, Jarlin 50
Garcia, Rico 94
Gausman, Kevin 52
Gott, Trevor 54
Harrison, Kyle 106
Hjelle, Sean 95, 105
Hwang, Jae-Gyun 85
Jhang, Jin-De 85
Kelly, Casey 96

La Stella, Tommy 24
Leone, Dominic 56
Littell, Zack 58
Longoria, Evan 26
Luciano, Marco 86, 99
Matos, Luis 87, 103
Menez, Conner 60, 106
Moronta, Reyes 96
Nunez, Dedniel 106
Pence, Hunter 88
Peralta, Wandy 62
Pinto, Ricardo 97
Posey, Buster 88
Ramos, Heliot 100
Rogers, Tyler 64
Ruf, Darin 28
Samardzija, Jeff 66
Schmitt, Casey 89, 106
Selman, Sam 68
Slater, Austin 30
Smoak, Justin 32
Solano, Donovan 34
Swiney, Nick 98
Toribio, Luis 90, 104
Tromp, Chadwick 36
Wade Jr, LaMonte 90
Watson, Tony 70
Webb, Logan 72
Wilson, Will 91, 102
Wisler, Matt 74
Wood, Alex 76

San Francisco Giants 2021

Yastrzemski, Mike 38

For the Joy of Keeping Score

THIRTY81 Project is an ongoing graphic design project focused on the ballparks of baseball. Since being established in 2013, scorecards have been a fundemental part of the effort. Each two-page card is uniquely ballpark-centric — there are 30 variants — and designed with both beginning and veteran scorekeepers in mind. Evolving over the years with suggestions from fans, broadcasters, and official scorers, the sheets are freely available to everyone as printable letter-size PDFs at the project webshop: www.THIRTY81Project.com

Download, Print, Score, Repeat ...

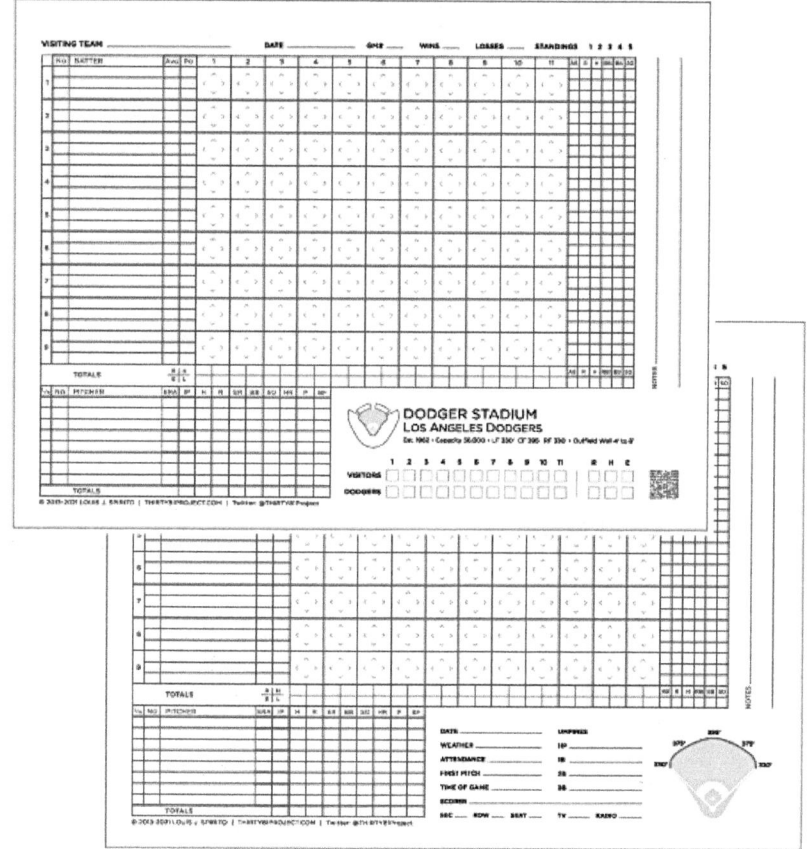

Scorecard design ©2013-2021 Louis J. Spirito | THIRTY81Project